The Tea Party

THE TEA
PARTY

RONALD P. FORMISANO

A BRIEF
HISTORY

THE JOHNS HOPKINS UNIVERSITY PRESS

BALTIMORE

© 2012 The Johns Hopkins University Press
All rights reserved. Published 2012
Printed in the United States of America on acid-free paper
9 8 7 6 5 4 3 2 1

The Johns Hopkins University Press
2715 North Charles Street
Baltimore, Maryland 21218-4363
www.press.jhu.edu

Library of Congress Cataloging-in-Publication Data

Formisano, Ronald P.
    The Tea Party : a brief history / Ronald P. Formisano.
        p. cm.
    Includes bibliographical references and index.
    ISBN-13: 978-1-4214-0596-4 (hdbk. : alk. paper)
    ISBN-13: 978-1-4214-0610-7 (electronic)
    ISBN-10: 1-4214-0596-2 (hdbk. : alk. paper)
    ISBN-10: 1-4214-0610-1 (electronic)
    1. Tea Party movement. 2. United States—Politics and
government—2009– I. Title.
    JK2391.T43F67 2012
    320.520973—dc23   2011042885

A catalog record for this book is available from the British Library.

Special discounts are available for bulk purchases of this book.
For more information, please contact Special Sales at 410-516-6936
or specialsales@press.jhu.edu.

The Johns Hopkins University Press uses environmentally friendly
book materials, including recycled text paper that is composed of at
least 30 percent post-consumer waste, whenever possible.

Contents

CONTENTS

Acknowledgments

THREE FRIENDS SET IN MOTION events that resulted in the writing of this book. Professor Tiziano Bonazzi of the University of Bologna, one of Italy's leading historians and theorists of American political culture, invited me to teach a course on Contemporary United States Politics at Bologna during the spring of 2011. When Dr. Robert J. Brugger, acquisitions editor at the Johns Hopkins University Press, learned that the course would have an emphasis on populism and that two weeks would be devoted to the Tea Party, he suggested that I write a short book on the Tea Party. Professor Anna Scacchi, an old friend, invited me to present a lecture on the Tea Party at the University of Padova, and I just kept expanding both the course material and the Padova lecture. Tiz, Bob, and Anna deserve my warmest thanks.

I am grateful also to my Italian and European students at Bologna for their interest in the politics of the United States, their sense of humor, and their willingness to adapt to my non-European teaching style. I hope some of them will enjoy the book.

Thanks also to Tina Hagee and Carol O'Reilly for technical assistance and to my research assistant Stephen Pickering. I enjoyed working with Martin Schneider, a demanding copy-editor. At a critical time during the summer of 2011 Deborah Bowman of the Chebeague Island Library and Melanie Gustafson and David Scrase provided crucial logistical support when I was flat on my back—literally. So too did Erica Chiquoine Formisano, who had to live under the same cottage roof for many days with an injured and (more than usually) grouchy spouse. Joe Conforti and John Zeugner, friends and fellow historians, read the manuscript at an early stage and provided helpful criticism and encouragement to run with it. Two readers for the Press not only turned in their comments within three days but also did not allow its unfinished state or the rapid schedule to hinder their delivery of constructive criticism. Their comments helped make this a better book. My children, Laura and Matthew—well, they always help just by being who they are.

INTRODUCTION

ON A COLD DECEMBER NIGHT IN 1773 some fifty to sixty men of the town of Boston, supported by virtually the entire community and by many people from surrounding towns, took action that in the space of about three hours changed the course of American history.

For seven and a half years before that episode on the Boston waterfront all the American colonies, but especially Massachusetts, had been at loggerheads with Britain as it sought to reorganize its empire and raise revenue from the mainland colonies. Americans were protesting their lack of representation in Parliament and challenged not only Britain's levying of taxes but also Parliament's broader assertions of sovereignty. The cycle of action and reaction that followed the "Boston Tea Party" led to the Declaration of Independence and the creation of the United States—even though Americans did not really celebrate the Boston Tea Party, or even call it that, until the 1820s and 1830s.

In the twenty-first century a right-wing populist movement has arisen—no, erupted—into the public arena and politics of the United States. It complains of high taxes and excessive government spending, and it has taken the name the Tea Party, where "Tea" stands for "Taxed Enough Already." It calls for—no, demands—limited government, debt reduction, no higher taxes, and no new spending. It reveres the Constitution, interpreting it as limiting the powers of the federal government, and argues that Congress has far exceeded its rightful boundaries.

It is too early to claim that the Tea Party has—or Tea Parties have—changed history, but the movement has had an enormous impact on the Republican Party, moving its center of gravity far to the right. It has severely constricted the maneuverability of the Obama administration and has shaped, perhaps more than any other current political force, the content of the nation's political agenda since 2009. The Tea Party is an umbrella that covers a loose confederation of grassroots groups as well as the corporate-funded offices of dedicated organizers who provide important infrastructure and guidance to the grassroots.

The movement's dedicated rank and file will tolerate no politics-as-usual compromise, moderate Republican lawmakers, or negotiation with political adversaries. This inflexibility—grassroots Tea Party leaders would call it "loyalty to principles"—has saturated the Republican congressional leadership and determined the positioning of most Republicans seeking national elective office in 2012. The salient fact: some 40 or even 45 percent of Republican primary voters are hard-core, no-compromise Tea Party supporters.

No one reading these pages is likely to be surprised to learn that the Tea Parties have attracted enormous media attention. Books have been written by cheerleaders and critics, newspapers and magazines regularly follow the movement's progress along with the cable news networks, and the internet brims with a veritable flood of material, much of it intensely partisan. This book intends to provide basic information about the Tea Party's origins, its significance, and its place in political history.

In our vast country the Tea Parties have attracted a dizzying array of groups and individuals, some of them from the fringes of public life seeking to exploit the Tea Party label. To complicate matters, the movement operates on several levels of activism. Although the brand has attracted and been exploited by free riders seeking publicity or profit, the people who have made a difference are angry and active on the grassroots level. This book aims to sort out the various components, to explore some of the movement's contradictions, and to understand it in relation to the powerful strain of historical populism in American political culture.

READING
TEA LEAVES

Many protest movements in our history have taken as their models some iconic event of the American Revolution, and the twenty-first-century Tea Party is not the first to associate itself with the Boston Tea Party of December 1773. But perhaps the more immediate template for the recent right-wing populist agitation comes from the successful 1976 film *Network,* a satirical dissection of television's obsession with ratings and winner of four Academy Awards. In the movie, an aging anchorman named Howard Beale (Peter Finch) is fired because his audience is dwindling. On his final broadcast he loses control and begins to shout, "I'm mad as hell, and I'm not going to take it anymore!" and urges his viewers to shout the same thing out of their windows—which many then do. His ratings immediately skyrocket, leading to his reinstatement; the "mad as hell" rant becomes his signature connection with his audience.

Astroturf or Grassroots Populism?

During 2009, as the newly elected administration of President Barack Obama pushed forward the Democrats' agenda for economic recovery and health care reform, a right-wing populist movement that was "mad as hell" emerged in passionate opposition to expanded government. It came to call itself the

Tea Party. By the end of 2010—particularly in the midterm elections of that year—the Tea Party had made a powerful impact on both the Democratic and Republican parties. Tea Party voters helped create the new Republican majority in the House of Representatives and during 2011 quickly exerted influence on the Republican legislative agenda. Indeed, the Tea Party, acting largely as a pressure group, has profoundly shaped the content of national political debate and has had a transforming impact on the Republican Party. On this narrative most observers agree.

Beyond that the Tea Party has provoked considerable debate among observers across the political spectrum. What is its significance? Is it a new kind of movement or a continuation of preexisting impulses? Is it manipulated by the Republican Party, or the other way around? Most observers agree that antigovernment and free market impulses animate its core ideology. Many of its supporters also favor the policies of the Religious Right, a key constituency of the Republican Party.

Superficially similar political uprisings have taken place throughout American history. From the early nineteenth century on, populist social movements and third parties have frequently upset the rhythm established by two major parties, challenging "politics as usual" while denouncing political parties, partisanship, and politicians. In this regard the Tea Party steps in well-worn footprints.

The main debate about the Tea Party, however, has to do with authenticity. To what extent has it emanated from the grassroots, from ordinary people, especially from those not previously involved in politics, or to what extent has it been created by corporations, billionaires, and right-wing media seeking to further their own agendas? Its partisans and critics alike, as if reading tea leaves, often see in it what they wish to see.[1]

When the Tea Party first appeared during 2009, critics—notably Democratic leaders—dismissed it as "astroturf populism." The term *astroturf* came into political use in the 1980s to describe grassroots activism that is more artificial than authentic. Usually it takes the form of lobbying by corporations who organize campaigns that are made to appear to be spontaneous mass activism but are actually front organizations with names that disguise their true purposes. Corporations that are heavy polluters, for example, may hire a public relations firm to create a fake organization that calls itself "Citizens for Clean Air and Water" and whose purpose is to lobby against the regulation of pollutants in air and water.

The speaker of the House of Representatives at the time, Nancy Pelosi, notably labeled the Tea Party "astroturf": "It's not really a grassroots movement. It's astroturf by some of the wealthiest people in America to keep the focus on tax cuts for the rich instead of for the great middle class." Not surprisingly, Tea Party activists at all levels of the movement rejected this description and criticized Pelosi—a Democrat already demonized by much of the right wing—as out of touch, or worse. They warned that Democrats—as well as Republicans—were underestimating the "people power" represented by the Tea Party.

By early 2010, President Obama himself—a much bigger target of Tea Party animosity than Speaker Pelosi—was making a distinction between the core of the movement and those outside the core who had "legitimate concerns." The core, he joked, probably would continue to believe he was a foreign-born socialist, but the "broader circle" of people around it "are legitimately concerned with the deficit ... [and] the federal government may be taking on too much."

The Tea Party can just as accurately be called the Tea Parties—both terms will be used here—because it exists on several levels and incorporates sometimes-competing factions as a loose confederation of sorts. As one friendly observer remarked, "There is no one main phone number [in Washington] for the Tea Parties." Polls show that roughly 25 to 30 percent or more of adults agree with or support the Tea Party; this amounts to tens of millions of citizens. An estimated 20 percent of self-identified Tea Party supporters are activists who attend rallies, donate money, and regularly follow the movement on the internet. Most of them are much angrier than other citizens about the direction the nation has taken.[2]

On a centralized, national level, simultaneously, are corporate-sponsored and well-funded organizations providing infrastructure support for Tea Party state and local networks. Political action committees interact with the corporate groups as well as the grassroots to mobilize rallies and protests and, above all, to contribute to the campaigns of Tea Party–favored Republicans.

So what is the answer to the question posed at the beginning of this chapter: "Astroturf or Grassroots Populism?" The simple answer is that the Tea Parties have been created by both kinds of populism, in part by the few—the corporate lobbyists from above—but also from the passionate many expressing real grassroots populism.

Both grassroots activism and corporate money have energized this right-wing populist rebellion. Grassroots passion and heavy corporate spending contributed to the Republican electoral successes in the 2010 midterm elections. But whether or not grassroots activists work with or accept sponsorship or support from corporate-backed national groups, they exude an attitude of fierce independence.

"The Tea Party believes the solutions to our country's problems lie within the Constitution and not partisan politics or corporate interests," wrote one Kentucky supporter to the *Lexington Herald Leader*. "We're well-informed adults who can form our own opinions and are sick of the culture of greed and corruption that exists in both government and business." That spirit of independence manifested itself in Arizona when Tea Party–courting Republican legislators passed a bill creating a "Don't Tread on Me" license plate design that Tea Party groups could use to raise money. The firmest opposition to the legislation came from Tea Partiers themselves, some of whom adamantly rejected the idea of accepting help from the state government. A few members liked the license plate scheme, but more agreed with activist Jim Wise, who said, "It goes against what we stand for, which is limited government."[3]

For many activists immersion in the Tea Party has represented a political awakening as well as a sense of fulfillment. Their voices were being heard; their actions, they now believed, were making a difference. Participation submerged their feelings of powerlessness and gave them what political scientists call a "sense of efficacy," a healthy mentality in a democratic republic. As for their political awareness, a recent poll found that Tea Party Republicans were paying much closer attention to the politicking leading up to the 2012 elections compared to non–Tea Party Republicans.

Before joining the movement David Kirkham of Utah had already experienced success and efficacy in his life and work. In 1995 he and his brother had started a company that built specialty cars, notably the 1960s Shelby Cobra—whose price tags now run from $100,000 to as much as $1 million. To learn to build these high-powered all-aluminum gems (and after seeing a Polish jet made of aluminum), Kirkham had learned Polish and traveled to Poland often. While making arrangements to have the bodies of the new cars made there, he saw some of the worst results of a state-controlled economy.

In 2008, immersed in his business and family life and nominally a libertarian and Republican, Kirkham was not politically active. But the bank bailouts begun under President

George W. Bush and the bailouts Obama undertook as well as the stimulus package galvanized him to take action. Socialism, he believed, was taking over. In March 2009, entirely on his own he called for a Tea Party rally in Salt Lake City. To his surprise about a hundred people showed up. Within months Kirkham was the head of the Utah Tea Party and hobnobbing with Republican political heavyweights like Utah's long-serving U.S. senator Orrin G. Hatch.[4] With Tea Party affairs now a large part of his life, political engagement meant acting to change the direction he feared the country was taking.

The relationship of grassroots activists with the Republican Party, however, has been typical of that of a fractious pressure group and has varied throughout different states and localities. In the 2010 congressional primaries Tea Party networks challenged many candidates anointed by the Republican establishment and replaced them with challengers the activists did not dismiss as "RINOs": Republicans in Name Only. Incumbents who were regarded as moderates on either cultural or economic issues or who had compromised or negotiated with Democrats faced a strong wave of Tea Party rejection. The reverberations from these battles continue to shape the positioning of Republicans seeking election in 2012.

Tea Partiers have worked with and against established Republican organizations, transforming the Republican Party in the process.

Fear of absorption by the GOP runs like a bright thread through the reactions of many movement activists to suggestions that the Tea Party should blend into the Republican Party. In many localities bitter contests pitted established Republican Party officeholders against Tea Party activists seeking to oust incumbents or move them to adopt the movement's agenda. In Bucks County, Pennsylvania, after a protracted and often frustrating struggle to take over Republican precinct committees and replace them with "people with our values," one local leader declared, "The only way to get rid of the Democrats is to get rid of the Republicans."[5]

Whatever setbacks Tea Party activists have suffered in conquering local Republican committees, members and supporters of the movement now virtually dominate the Republican voting base and in 2012 may constitute 40 percent or more of Republican primary voters. Amazingly, 10 percent of all voters regard themselves as Tea Party members first and Republicans second.[6]

Liberal critics of the Tea Party have underestimated the degree to which frustration with the Republican Party in the closing years of the Bush administration contributed to the rise of the Tea Party. Indeed, about half of Tea Party activists hold an unfavorable view of the Republican Party. As one conservative blogger put it, "Disenchantment with the Republican Party under our 'compassionate conservative' president George W. Bush which overcame legions of conservatives was the initial inspiration that gave rise to the Tea Party." Frustration with "the GOP's betrayal of the values" the Tea Party affirms causes a majority of its supporters, he claimed, to "refuse to explicitly or formally identify with the Republican Party."[7]

Disenchantment with the Bush administration and congressional Republicans helped to generate the central complaints of the movement: federal government spending, the government's soaring debt, and the increasing size of government. As critics of the party point out, Tea Party public protests did not emerge until after the Bush administration had left office. Once President Obama entered the Oval Office, Tea Party rallies, marches, and pronouncements focused like a laser beam on those core issues.

In a 2010 Gallup poll measuring "Extremely Serious Threats to Future U.S. Wellbeing" 61 percent of Tea Party supporters identified the federal debt as the most serious threat, compared to 44 percent of those neutral to the movement and 29 percent of its opponents. Tea Partiers ranked the size and power of the federal government as almost as great a threat as terrorism, 51 and 49 percent, respectively.[8]

"The size of government" can refer to many things, but however it is interpreted the federal government has grown since the mid-twentieth century under both Democratic and Republican presidents and Congresses. Many conservatives, expecting that the Bush administration would limit government growth, instead recoiled from its contribution to this long-term process. The 9/11 attack on the United States soon after Bush took office had much to do with the expansion of government over the next decade. The "war on terror" and the invasions of Afghanistan and Iraq, in the words of the authoritative British magazine the *Economist,* "led to the biggest expansion in the American state since Lyndon Johnson's in the mid-1960s." The new Department of Homeland Security became the largest new bureaucracy created since World War II. Then Bush oversaw a huge extension of the Medicare prescription drug benefit at a cost of $62 billion a year and more federal intervention and control over education across the country. Hundreds of millions went to Homeland Security grants, local firefighting grants, healthy marriage promotion, and abstinence education. While selectively dismantling environmental and other regulations for favored industries, the administration actually added seven thousand new pages of federal regulations.[9]

In 2011 the federal government directly employed just over 2.8 million persons, reflecting steady overall growth in the number employed with some intervals of decline. During recent decades state and local governments have increased more rapidly than the national government. But according to social scientists, the "true size of [the federal] government" must take into account "the largely hidden" workforce that the government employs through grants and contracts. If one takes those figures into account, the number of federal employees has swelled by an additional several million.[10]

But these figures and additional ways of measuring government size—the most common is expenditures as a proportion of gross domestic product—perhaps mean little. While the Tea Parties and conservatives generally believe that "big government" stunts economic growth, social scientists disagree about the relationship of government size to prosperity. What matters rather are citizens' perceptions and how the federal government intersects at various points in the lives of its citizens: such as on April 15, or during air travel since 9/11, or with regulations that require small businesses to make expensive modifications in their physical plants.

For the Tea Party the umbrella terms are *big government* and *spending*. In the Gallup poll measuring perceived threats to the nation's well-being, 80 percent of Tea Party supporters said that the government is doing too much that should be left to individuals and businesses (only 27% of Tea Party opponents agreed, and 64% of that group believed government should be doing more to solve the country's problems). Tea Party activists are quite adamant—92 percent—about rejecting government as a way to solve problems or meet needs. "The government is doing too much" is a phrase that easily encompasses "spending" and "big government."

The economic collapse of 2008 forced the Bush administration to intervene massively in the nation's financial system with the hundreds of billions of dollars conveyed through the Troubled Asset Relief Program. During 2009 the Obama administration continued the bailout of banks and financial institutions—entities seen by the great majority of Americans as bearing great responsibility for the crisis—and then moved to aid the auto industry. The Democrats also pushed forward with an approximately $800 billion package to stimulate the economy, although a healthy chunk of that "spending" consisted of tax reductions. *But the government was doing too much.*

By early 2011 the general public had moved closer to Tea Party attitudes regarding government. A January poll found that 67 percent of American adults were somewhat (29%) or very (38%) dissatisfied with the "size and power of the federal government." In late March 58 percent agreed that that the government had "too much power." Americans also showed they had been paying attention to the roots of the financial and economic crisis, however, with large majorities seeing too much power in the hands of lobbyists (71%), major corporations (67%), and financial institutions (67%).[11]

At the same time, while a great many Americans now share much of the Tea Party's discontent with government, when it comes to the expensive core government entitlements of Medicare, Medicaid, and Social Security, decided majorities want to keep them as they are. Huge majorities (77% to 87%) say these programs have been "good for the country." When asked if reducing the budget is more important than keeping benefits as they are, the adults surveyed answered by a margin of 60 to 32 percent to retain the status quo. A similar majority (61% to 31%) opposed obliging people on Medicare to pay more "to make it financially secure."[12]

Pollsters have found contradictory tendencies like these for some time among the American citizenry: a generalized discontent that "the government is doing too much" alongside an unwillingness to change or cut large and expensive programs deemed essential to their well-being. Public opinion trackers have reported for some time that the American electorate is ideologically conservative and programmatically liberal. Significantly, while Democrats overwhelmingly favor keeping Social Security and Medicare unchanged, Republicans are closely divided, with a plurality (47% to 44%)

agreeing with Democrats in wanting to keep those programs as they are. This divide exists not only within the Republican Party but also, as will be seen, within the Tea Parties.

Another fault line in the movement to be examined here is the gap between the goals of the corporate money men and Republican operatives and those of the grassroots supporters. Disagreement has arisen also between the libertarian and evangelical wings of the Tea Parties. These relationships are still evolving.

Parties, Anti-Parties, and Populism

Not quite an independent political party and not quite a full-fledged populist social movement but having some characteristics of both, where does the Tea Party fit in the broad sweep of American political history? Third parties and populist movements have emerged to challenge the status quo throughout our past. No doubt many grassroots Tea Partiers see themselves as following in that rebellious tradition.

In the wake of the American Revolution rural folk often mobilized to take action against new state governments and policies that favored urban elites and mercantile interests. In the 1780s, as the Revolutionary War ended, angry farmers from Maine to the Carolinas engaged in vigilantism and extralegal and illegal resistance to protest unfair state economic policies. These protests, usually conducted in the name of "the people," favored decentralized government and local control. During the country-wide debate over the adoption of the new United States framework of government in 1787 and 1788 opponents (known as the Anti-Federalists) feared establishment of a too-powerful government removed from ordinary people and favoring "aristocracy." After the adoption of the federal constitution in 1789, populist protest tended to take on an antistatist character, quick to defy both the federal and state governments. Frequent mobilizations of local communities to fight externally imposed policies seen as unjust continued a pattern set during the Revolution.[13]

Among the best known of these chronic episodes of popular defiance was the Whiskey Rebellion. In the 1790s in western Pennsylvania small distillers and farmers engaged in vigilante resistance against a federal excise tax on ardent spirits, prompting President George Washington to send an army larger than any he had commanded in the Revolution on a punitive expedition. But the suppression of the "Whiskey Rebels" in Pennsylvania hardly ended vigilantism in the new republic—the resistance to the excise tax continued in regions beyond Pennsylvania. And rebellious Kentuckians and Carolinians, among others, never saw Washington's army.

After 1800 on the eastern frontier region of Massachusetts, later the state of Maine, settlers thinly disguised as "Indians" à la the Boston Tea Party drove off the sheriffs and agents of large landlords who claimed ownership of their farms. Needless to say, these close-to-the-land Americans did not have the blessings or monetary backing of the equivalent of big businessmen of their day. Far from it; they saw the wealthy land owners and the financial and commercial interests (who wanted "the people" to know their place and stay in it) as their oppressors.

In the 1830s the political arena took on a recognizably modern form, with two major political parties gradually emerging within an institutionalized political system. Although vigilantism never really ended, many populist social movements thereafter turned to the ballot box or organized as third parties, often attracting just enough votes to influence the balance of power between the two major parties and thereby force one or the other to respond to their agenda.

From the 1850s through the twenty-first century two major parties dominated most national and state elections, while independent political movements and parties, often ephemeral, flourished at the state and local level. Of course third parties frequently mounted powerful challenges to the major parties and often made a lasting impact on policy: the Know Nothing or American Republican Party of the 1850s, the new Republican Party that emerged in the 1850s and became the major party opposition to the Democrats, the People's Party of the 1890s, the Socialist Party and Theodore Roosevelt's Progressive Party of 1912, the Progressive Party of 1924, the Dixiecrats of 1948, George Wallace's American Independent Party of 1968, and Ross Perot's Reform Party of 1992.

In many instances, third and independent parties throughout our past have, in a fashion adopted by the Tea Party, proclaimed themselves to be anti-party parties—or not parties at all. They have declared opposition to parties themselves, regarding the leaders and members of the major political parties as under the spell of partisan loyalty and thus heedless of the people's interests. Anti-party parties often organize in imitation of the established parties, but they nonetheless maintain that they adhere to principle, that is, they disclaim any motivation from reasons of patronage, group interest, or personal gain.

The Tea Party grassroots shares some of the classic hallmarks of the third-party/independent tradition: suspicion of professional politicians, frustration with the two-party system and politics as usual, and a hankering for simple solutions to complex problems. They claim to be above the nitty-gritty of politics and the established parties and proudly declare their unwillingness to negotiate or compromise.

The Tea Party's various elements, unlike independent third parties of the past, have thus far acted primarily as a pressure group within just one party—the Republican Party. In the 1890s, by contrast, the People's Party brought together a diverse coalition of farmers' organizations, labor unionists,

temperance reformers, prohibitionists, women's rights advo-
cates, and other progressives to challenge the new economic
power of industrial and financial capitalism, having found
the Republican and Democratic parties to be unresponsive
to their needs and too beholden to moneyed interests.

In 1892 the People's Party proposed a radical—but not
anti-capitalist—platform of reform: a graduated income tax,
direct election of U.S. Senators by popular vote (state legislatures had elected them since 1789), government regulation
or ownership of railroads and the telegraph, currency in-
flation, and other measures requiring action by the federal
government to redress inequities in the economic and political systems. The Populists were not anti-capitalists because
the large and small farmers and rural commercial interests
making up the majority of their coalition wanted to keep their
farms and rural businesses—with the national government
helping them to help themselves.[14]

The Populists recognized that a wholly new system of
industrial-financial power had come into being and that it
was diminishing their liberties and capacities as free citizens. They realized that the Jeffersonian classical-liberal
tradition of limited government left them at the mercy of
consolidated capital, and they called upon government to intervene to restore the American promise of equal economic
opportunity—not an equality of results but an equality of
process. A keystone of their platform was the sub-treasury
system by which the government would provide farmers
credit, not welfare, and store their crops when the market was
depressed. Much as Americans do today, they faced economic
forces beyond their control. So they turned to the central
government to restore balance to the political and economic
system.

The Populists did not mince words in accusing the
industrial-capitalist elite of controlling the political system.

They declared that all branches of government had been cor-
rupted by money and that the neglect of the Democratic and
Republican parties had caused "the fruits of the toil of millions" to be "badly stolen to build up colossal fortunes for a few,
unprecedented in the history of mankind; and the possessions
of these, in turn, despise the Republic and endanger liberty."
Therefore they believed that "the power of government—in
other words, of the people—should be expanded."[15]

In its political strategy the People's Party adjusted to the
political balance of power in different states, cooperating
with Democrats or Republicans or remaining independent
according to their calculation of what would bring electoral
success. In contrast, the Tea Party has worked only within
the Republican Party, acting primarily as a pressure group
seeking to influence the party's policies and its selection of
candidates. It also has enjoyed the patronage of powerful and
wealthy allies in corporate America. The progressive rebels
of the 1890s, who proudly embraced the term *populist* and
bequeathed it to our political vocabulary, would have been
astonished if any of the titans of Wall Street of their day, men
they regarded as "robber barons" and "plutocrats," had supported their cause with rivers of cash.

Widespread populist episodes from the American Revolution to the early twentieth century differ from contemporary
populist movements in that they grew out of local communities, drawing sustenance from churches, towns, families and
kin networks, unions, and fraternal and women's and other
associations. These kinds of bonds operate today in forming
the Tea Parties, but transcontinental cooperation depends
heavily on technology, telephones, computers, and of course
the internet.

Today's Tea Parties differ in significant ways from late-
nineteenth- and early-twentieth-century reformers in opposing the use of government power for social ends; in visceral

hostility to federal taxation; in antipathy to labor unions; in preference for the free market rather than fairness for all; in opposition to programs to help the needy; and, generally, in a reactionary crusade to roll back federal power. Like other right-wing populist movements, the Tea Parties have produced leaders who tend to display a macho persona, and the grassroots sometimes seem unwilling to tolerate the expression of opposing political views.

But the Tea Parties, like other right-wing populisms of the past, also share features with progressive populist movements. The Tea Parties' grassroots resemble past progressive populisms in being pervaded by anti-elite sentiment. The Tea Parties often denounce political elites, much as the Populists denounced the political class of their day.

Deep within the political views of grassroots Tea Party supporters, according to a recent Harvard University study, lies an outlook closely resembling a central theme of historical progressive populism—producerism. For much of American history reformers separated society into the "toiling masses" or the producing many in opposition to the nonproductive but powerful and wealthy few. They defined their enemies not in terms of Marxist class warfare but rather as the parasites of economic society, the idle rich, the absentee owners but not the resident owner of an enterprise, dishonest lawyers, saloon keepers, financiers who gambled with other people's money—in short, the nonproducers.

Tea Party members, according to this study, "judge entitlement programs not in terms of abstract free-market orthodoxy, but according to perceived deservingness of recipients." Thus Tea Partiers do not so much see a conflict between big government and the freedom-loving individual but between "workers" and "people who don't work." "Freeloaders" here includes the young; naturally, this includes the sons and daughters of some older respondents.

Most of this study's research was conducted in Massachusetts, which has low levels of illegal immigration, especially compared with states with foreign borders. Nevertheless Tea Partiers in this famously blue state passionately condemned illegal immigrants as particularly offensive freeloaders. In this they agree with Tea Party supporters across the country, 83 percent of whom in 2010 saw illegal immigration as a serious problem—more than other Republicans and Americans overall.[16]

It should be noted that labor leaders and reformers of the late nineteenth and early twentieth centuries complained of the effect of illegal and cheap foreign labor on the standard of living of American workers. But resonant as contemporary conservatives' freeloader theme may be with historically progressive producerism, it is a narrower and more restricted version.

At about the time the Harvard study received media attention, so too did the grim news that the nation's jobless rate had gone up the previous month. The official numbers were 14 million unemployed and 9.2 percent of the workforce. But as with the "true size" of government the real number of those without work, according to many economists, is much higher. Over time many of the unemployed stop looking for work and go unrecorded by the official statistics. The true total of unemployed probably easily exceeds 15 million, a figure that does not include an additional 15 million or more Americans who are underemployed.

These fellow Americans do not seem to be a target of grassroots Tea Partiers' displeasure—nor of their concern. Tea Party and other Republicans in Congress, however, have opposed extending unemployment benefits to the long-term unemployed. Tea Party political leaders and conservatives argue that extending benefits beyond ninety-nine weeks creates dependency and prolongs unemployment. They claim that almost two years of benefits "changes the behavior of the . . . unemployed." One conservative economist wrote that the long period of benefits is "almost like a drug addiction."

Many of the unemployed bitterly resent this notion. According to the latest data, it now takes an average of nine months to find a new job after losing one. For many, of course, the true length of time to find new work has been much longer. Doug Yocum, a sixty-year-old college graduate who suffered a stroke at the age of fifty-four, causing him to lose his savings and then to search for new work, lost his new construction company job in 2008 and has been unemployed ever since. He sends out many resumes every week but knows that his age and ruined credit score are working against him. He is insulted by the idea that $400 a week in unemployment benefits have kept him from looking for work or that it resembles drug addiction. He wonders what critics of extended benefits would think if they were in his shoes.

Ironically, those without work, lacking institutions through which to express their grievances, have mounted no populist protest. They vote at much lower rates (in 2010, 35% of the jobless voted, compared to 46% of working citizens). But the right-wing populist protest now occupying center stage in American politics concentrates on other problems facing the nation.[17]

Throughout American history populist movements have mobilized either progressive or reactionary impulses, with many combining elements of both kinds. Many different kinds of individuals have claimed to be populists, declaring themselves men or women of the people, for the people. Whether progressive or reactionary, populist movements, parties, and leaders protest that "politics has escaped popular control" and that we the people "have been shut out of power by corrupt politicians and an unrepresentative elite who betray our interests, ignore our opinions, and treat us with contempt."[18]

The Tea Parties stand in the long tradition of this kind of protest. In contemporary American politics, however, populist claims have become diluted because they saturate not only politics but commerce and entertainment too. A prominent political scientist put it well when he said that populism is "everywhere in American politics, and nowhere in particular."[19] No matter how wealthy, as candidates, most politicians adopt a populist mantle and offer themselves as "just regular" and once elected quickly display their lack of authenticity. Well aware of this pattern, Tea Partiers express their frustration with what has become a "political class" comparable to that in European countries, a sentiment shared by many other Americans.

Although the loosely confederated Tea Parties at the grassroots level exhibit elements of historic populist protest, their complex interaction with wealth deserves close attention.

THE RISE

of the

TEA PARTY

THROUGHOUT THE MANY ACCOUNTS of the Tea Party's origins there exists what might be termed the search for the Rosa Parks moment. In 1955 Rosa Parks sparked a pivotal turn in the modern civil rights movement—the Montgomery, Alabama, bus boycott—by refusing to move to the back of a bus. Meaning no disrespect to the heroic Parks, many historians have shown that the civil rights movement of the 1950s and 1960s was long in preparation and had multiple origins. Other brave women had taken similar but unheralded actions in the years before. Moreover, Rosa Parks did not come out of nowhere. She had been secretary of her local chapter of the National Association for the Advancement of Colored People and had recently attended a school in Tennessee devoted to promoting racial equality and workers' rights. But her refusal to obey the white bus driver was impulsive; she was, as she said, "tired of giving in."

The Search for the Rosa Parks Moment

So it is with the Tea Party. Seemingly spontaneous individual protests against the Obama administration's programs to rescue the economy and other policies emerged from the grassroots across the country from Seattle to Florida, and yet the Tea Party has felt a need to locate the equivalent of Rosa Parks—a single individual who seemingly out of nowhere suddenly made a huge difference. The search has generated several candidates. Some Tea Party leaders have nominated Mary Rakovitch, a former electrical engineer in the auto industry who was laid off in her fifties. On February 10, 2009, Rakovitch, her husband, and several others appeared as protesters outside a town hall meeting in Fort Myers, Florida, that featured President Obama and Florida governor Charlie Crist. Rakovitch told reporters that they had shown up to object to government spending and waste and Obama's promotion of socialism, though "he doesn't call it that"; soon she was appearing on Fox News with Neil Cavuto.

Rakovitch later explained that she had discovered FreedomWorks, a corporate organization promoting the movement and providing activists with infrastructure, on the internet and learned that it would be holding a two-and-a-half-hour "training session" in her area in early January 2009 about how to protest government spending. In the wake of her fifteen minutes of fame and a firmly entrenched place in the early history of the Tea Party Rakovitch brimmed with satisfaction at having done something important.

Among other candidates for first to launch the Tea Party one of the most interesting is Keli Carender, a thirty-year-old conservative blogger from Seattle who organized a "Porkulus Protest," borrowing the term "Porkulus" from Rush Limbaugh, to denounce Obama's stimulus bill to revive the economy. Carender, who goes by "Liberty Belle" on her blog, teaches basic math to adult learners and acts in an improv group on weekends; her fiancé voted for Obama. Carender's event, which drew about 120 people with help from syndicated conservative columnist Michelle Malkin, took place on February 16, President's Day, the day before Obama signed

the stimulus package. By April she had succeeded in mobiliz-
ing twelve hundred people to attend a Tax Day Tea Party. A
year later FreedomWorks flew her and sixty others regarded
as national leaders to Washington for a training session.[1]

Carender and Rakovitch testify to the pull of the Tea Party
for ordinary people, some, like Rakovitch, previously unin-
volved politically, others, like Carender, already strongly
engaged in conservative activism. But their claims as "the
first" are undercut by multiple antecedents.

In fact, corporate lobbyists had been suggesting antitax
and antiregulatory Tea Parties for several years, and at least
one candidate for the Republican presidential nomination
had held a fundraising tea party event in 2007.

Most accounts, however, focus on February 19, 2009, and
a "Howard Beale"–style outburst by CNBC financial reporter Rick Santelli on the floor of the Chicago Mercantile
Exchange. In an "I'm mad as hell" moment Santelli exploded
into a rant in which he criticized the Obama administration's
plan to refinance mortgages. He complained that the program
rewarded "bad behavior" and "losers" and suggested holding
a "Chicago tea party" in which traders would dump derivatives in the Chicago River.

Santelli directed his anger, interestingly, at the low-
income house buyers who had been scammed into taking on
mortgages they could not afford rather than at the banks and
investment firms that, by creating derivatives, had made huge
bets on the failure of those mortgages—and then profited
when they did fail. *Playboy* magazine suggested that Santelli's
supposedly impromptu diatribe was carefully orchestrated by
right-wing lobbyists.

FreedomWorks and its predecessor Americans for
Prosperity—entities funded by corporate billionaires—had
been floating the idea of antitax, antigovernment tea party
rallies for several years before 2009.[2] On December 16, 2007,

libertarian congressman Ron Paul, trying to raise money for his campaign for the Republican presidential nomination, had held a symbolic tea party in Boston—collecting more than $6 million, the largest single sum any candidate had raised, to that point, in one day. By early 2009 suggestions for tea party protests came both before and after President Obama's inauguration. Several originated in a network of stock market traders connected to FedUpUSA, a pro-business, antigovernment lobbying group. The Illinois Libertarian Party around that time was talking about holding a Boston Tea Party in Chicago and later claimed it "gave Rick Santelli the idea." On February 11, a Fox Business Network personality appeared on the morning show *Fox and Friends* waving tea bags and saying, "It's time for a tea party."[3]

What mattered more than Santelli's rant was its promulgation by right-wing bloggers across the internet and its repeated replays on the Fox Network. Within hours, too, FreedomWorks and similar Washington-based groups realized that their moment had come, that the economic meltdown and the change from a Republican to a Democratic administration had created the climate to launch into Tea Party organizing. In early 2009 economic, political, and cultural shocks came together to activate ordinary persons across the country—mostly conservative Republicans, but also independents and others—to organize and mobilize. The internet, by now a routine element of political campaigning, was essential to the rise of the Tea Party.

Media and Money

On April 15, 2009, "Tax Day," Tea Party demonstrators reportedly gathered in some 750 towns and cities across the country. The largest, in Atlanta, attracted several thousand. Similar demonstrations occurred on July 4.

A powerful media engine promoted these protests: the Fox News cable network, owned by right-wing billionaire Rupert Murdoch and run by former Republican campaign manager Roger Ailes. Fox News relentlessly urged its viewers to get involved in the April 15 "Tax Day" protests. Its various personalities, led by its superstar "hosts" Glenn Beck, Sean Hannity, Bill O'Reilly, and others, urged viewers on dozens of occasions to attend the rallies. Beginning in February 2009, shortly after Santelli's rant, the talking heads on Fox News repeatedly declared that a storm of protest was gathering throughout the country against the Obama administration's economic policies.

On the April 6 edition of America's Newsroom, for example, over a chyron that declared "Tea Party USA Growing Revolution" and "Tea Party Protesters Angry at Trillions in Government Spending," Andrea Tantaros said, "People are fighting back against Barack Obama's radical shift to turn us into Europe."

That same day Glenn Beck suggested that viewers could celebrate the protests by watching Fox News or by showing up at cities where he and fellow Fox News hosts Neil Cavuto, Greta Van Susteren, and Sean Hannity would be "live" at the demonstrations. While Beck spoke, a chyron labeled the rallies "FNC Tax Day Tea Parties." Fox also offered viewers websites with links to Tea Party organizers and repeated reminders of the times and locations in the major cities involved. From April 6 to April 14 Fox News featured at least twenty commentaries on the protests and 107 commercial promotions.[4]

Glenn Beck's importance to all of this cannot be emphasized enough. No right-wing radio or TV talk show host exceeded Beck in negative hyperbole directed at President Obama and at progressives, liberals, and Democrats. President Obama, he once said, "hates white people," a statement he subsequently retracted. Beck quickly became a hero for many Tea Partiers; early surveys found that they "deeply identify" with and trust him. Most importantly, in countless ways Beck stimulated fear of government among his viewers.

Indeed, night after night Beck warned viewers about the socialist takeover of the federal government that, he said, had been decades in the making, put in motion initially by Progressives like Theodore Roosevelt and Woodrow Wilson in the early twentieth century. Beck equated Progressives with liberals, socialists, Communists, and even Fascists, and he charged that they had stolen "our history to separate us from our Constitution and God." A former radio disc jockey, recovered alcoholic, and convert to Mormonism, Beck drew heavily on the grandiose right-wing conspiracy theories of Communist takeover current during the Cold War and propounded by the late right-wing writer W. Cleon Skousen and those of the John Birch Society founded by Robert Welch in 1958. Welch believed in a Communist conspiracy so insidious that Republican president Dwight Eisenhower, Supreme Commander of Allied Forces in World War II, had become its "conscious dupe." Beck even found inspiration in centuries-old conspiracy theories, but whatever his source, he pounded home the message that the United States was on the road to totalitarianism. His views hardly represented those of Tea Party organizations or of all Tea Party supporters, but they did penetrate into the movement's ranks.[5]

A week before the Tax Day rallies, however, Murdoch pulled Beck from the Atlanta protest and issued a statement saying that Fox News should not be supporting the Tea Party "or any other party," a rather bewildering action given subsequent events. On April 15 Sean Hannity appeared at the Atlanta rally while Beck went to San Antonio. Greta Van Susteren camped out with cameras in front of the White House. She interviewed Tea Party activists and Republican South

Carolina governor Mark Sanford. Neil Cavuto broadcast live from the Sacramento rally surrounded by Tea Partiers and proclaimed that, just as the original Boston Tea Party was about "taxation without representation" so too was this protest because, even though Barack Obama had been voted into office, voters had not voted for his economic policies.

The Tea Party's most significant political noise, though, came in August 2009 when, spurred on and transported by FreedomWorks and other corporate entities, Tea Party activists appeared at local congressional town hall meetings being held for representatives to discuss the Democrats' health insurance legislation. Instead of allowing Congressmen to answer questions, however, "outraged" activists did their best to disrupt the meetings. Although coached to do so from above, the militants needed little prodding to shout and scream. The antigovernment mood ventured into the absurd when protesters shouted, "Keep your government hands off my Medicare!" But critics who focused on illogical complaints were missing the point: this was political theater staged to create the impression of the unpopularity of health insurance reform.

On September 12 the Tea Party faithful gathered in Washington, D.C., for a protest march from Freedom Plaza to the Capitol. By now the Fox News cheerleaders had turned to their blogs to promote the event. On its website, Fox News declared "Tea Party Express Takes Washington by Storm."

A crowd unofficially estimated by D.C. officials at a minimum of seventy-five thousand carried signs denouncing big government, high taxes, "socialism," abortion, President Obama, and health care reform. Former congressman and lobbyist Dick Armey, now of FreedomWorks, was a featured speaker, along with Senator Jim DeMint of South Carolina, who had earned the nickname "Senator Tea Party." Some marchers carried racially offensive posters of President

Obama, depicting him, for example, as an African witch doctor. Some adorned Obama's visage with a Hitler mustache while labeling him a Communist or Muslim, embarrassing some of the other attendees, who found such messages inappropriate and counterproductive.

Further excessive behavior surfaced in Washington over the weekend of March 20, 2010, when Congress passed the new health law. Several Tea Party demonstrators called black congressmen "nigger" and spat on one of them; gay congressman Barney Frank was called a "faggot" and a "homo," and Jewish representatives also heard anti-Semitic slurs.

Pragmatic Tea Party activists try to discourage such offensive behavior for practical reasons as well as out of conviction. But no Tea Party official or group apologized for the abuse meted out to congressmen by their members or allies. Instead, those defenders of the Tea Party who addressed the matter denied that these incidents had even happened, thus impugning the credibility of the congressmen who had been the objects of the attacks (among them the civil rights hero John Lewis, who had endured far worse in his life). To his credit, Congressman Heath Shuler, a conservative, white Democrat from North Carolina, made a point of testifying to the truth of their accounts.

During this same outburst of anger by demonstrators against the new health law, a small group of them accosted an older man in a wheelchair who was debilitated by Parkinson's disease and who had come to support the legislation and showered him with insults. One man threw dollar bills on him. Captured on video, that particular act of cruelty followed the bill thrower back to his city and local media; he apologized a week later, saying he had "just snapped."

Other incidents illustrated the pragmatism of Tea Party activists. The Iowa Tea Party chairman is Ryan Rhodes; he is under thirty, politically savvy, and poised to play a role in presidential politics as would-be Republican presidential nominees court Iowans in 2012. When a splinter Tea Party group put up a billboard in Mason City that depicted President Obama with Adolf Hitler and Vladimir Lenin, Rhodes led the campaign to take it down.[6]

On August 28, 2010, when a Glenn Beck–promoted Washington rally took place, drawing over one hundred thousand people, the speakers delivered no angry rhetoric to the crowd, with the tone set by Beck himself—who had labeled the event "Restore Honor." His address sounded more like a sermon than a political speech; he proclaimed, perhaps to the puzzlement of many in the audience expecting something different, that "America today begins to turn back to God." Former Alaska governor, 2008 vice presidential candidate, and Tea Party favorite Sarah Palin injected a brief political note, warning of the threat of socialism, but she too stuck to nonpartisan themes. That the rally took place at the Lincoln Memorial on the anniversary of Martin Luther King's 1963 speech produced much pre-rally controversy, along with a much smaller counterdemonstration protesting that Beck was "hijacking" King's legacy. Having apologized for his remark that President Obama hated white people, Beck now said he objected to Obama's "liberation theology."

Fox News also faithfully covered the bus tours and rallies organized by the Tea Party Express, a faux-grassroots venture funded by a political action committee called Our Country Deserves Better, which was originally formed in 2008 to elect Republican John McCain president. Sal Russo, a Republican political operative since the 1960s and the wealthy head of a consulting firm, pumped more than $4.5 million into McCain's campaign, then in 2009 transformed his PAC into the Tea Party Express. It launched bus tours with country singers and Republican celebrities as prominent as Palin. In 2010 Russo's PAC spent heavily on attack ads and campaign contributions on behalf of Tea Party–backed candidates. The Express gave nearly $1 million to Republican candidate Sharron Angle to defeat Senate majority leader Harry Reid of Nevada, nearly $350,000 to elect Scott Brown senator of Massachusetts, and a similar amount for the Tea Party candidate in Delaware. The Express proved profitable for Russo and his consulting firm. Of $1.3 million in expenditures from July to November, a little more than $857,000 went to Russo, Marsh, and Associates.[7]

While the Tea Party Express nevertheless contributed heavily to candidates' campaigns and provided publicity for grassroots activists' rallies and protests, an affiliated organization, the Tea Party Patriots, represented a decentralized network of independent activists operating across the country in dozens of smaller groups. The Patriots claimed to have 2,800 local cells in their network, but a *Washington Post* inquiry could identify just 1,400 separate groups and was able to contact only 647. Another source credited the Patriots with 115,311 online members, 63 percent of whom were male.

The Tea Party Patriots, the most grassroots entity among tea party organizations (and is so regarded by other Tea Party groups), distrusted and resented the Tea Party Express. For some Patriot activists Russo and his PAC suggested cooptation by the Republican Party. Thus some Patriots referred to the Express as the "Astroturf Express" and even issued a press release in April 2010 disassociating their organization from the Express. At the time the Express's chairman, Mark Williams, had been making a string of racially offensive remarks, which the Patriots believed were giving all Tea Partiers a bad name. He was promptly relieved of his duties. The Patriots also saw the Express as draining money from the grassroots. Donors who gave to the Express usually did not realize they were giving to a PAC, said a Patriots activist, and "that hurts local grass-roots tea party organizers."[8]

The California Tea Party Patriots published a lengthy statement to declare its lack of connection with the Tea Party Express. The Californians charged that it had jumped "on the tea party bandwagon." Although sensitive to being manipulated, the Patriots' scattered network of enthusiasts nevertheless worked selectively with other astroturf groups. It held itself ready to respond to certain calls from above—calls issued by organizers paid by corporate money—to mobilize for protests.

Intertwined as the Fox News Corporation was with the Tea Party during its explosive growth in 2009, when the 2010 midterm elections approached Fox News became as much or more integrated with the Republican Party. The mission of Fox, indeed, appeared to be to fold the Tea Party into the GOP.

During 2010 the influential array of Fox News hosts led by Beck, Hannity, and Cavuto began promoting an alliance if not a merger between the Tea Party and the Republican Party. By the spring of that year, according to the watchdog Media Matters, thirty or more Fox News personalities had endorsed, raised money, or campaigned for Republican candidates in over 600 instances. By April Fox hosts and contributors had raised $2.5 million for Republican candidates.

By August 2010 Rupert Murdoch's dictum of 2009 that the FNC should not be supporting the Tea Party "or any other party" was a distant memory. Fox News dropped all pretense when it donated a million dollars to the Republican Governor's Association and another million dollars to the U.S. Chamber of Commerce, which had announced its intention to fund candidates opposed to the Obama administration agenda. Questioned about the seeming inconsistency between these donations and Fox News's insistence on non-partisanship, a spokesman commented that the "News Corporation believes in the power of free markets, and the RGA's pro-business agenda supports our priorities at this most critical time in our economy."

To critics, the unspoken alliance between the two groups was finally confirmed. Comedian Stephen Colbert, referencing the popular singer Beyoncé, mused that the longtime flirtation between the Republican Party and Fox News was now officially a marriage: "They put a ring on it and it's about time." Fellow Comedy Channel satirist Jon Stewart was more direct: "If anything, the Republicans should be paying Fox News millions and millions of dollars."

The alliance was difficult to miss. By the autumn four of the five major potential Republican candidates for president at the time were on the network's payroll as commentators (Mike Huckabee, Newt Gingrich, Sarah Palin, and Rick Santorum). Only Mitt Romney failed to make the Fox News payroll—not because of his independent money but because Murdoch strongly opposed him.

As governor of Massachusetts Romney had overseen passage of a health insurance plan that later became a rough model for the Democrats' Affordable Care Act. That connection of course generated considerable hostility to Romney among right-wing Republicans. In May 2011, as Romney delivered a speech intended to distance himself from Obama and defend his state plan as "good for Massachusetts," Murdoch's *Wall Street Journal* lambasted him for his "troubling failure of political understanding and principle." That "fatal flaw," the paper suggested, left Romney better suited to be President Obama's running mate than his Republican opponent. Liberal bloggers also reported that the libertarian billionaire brothers David and Charles Koch, funders of Tea Party supportive groups behind the scenes, shared Murdoch's hostility to Romney.

Throughout the campaign season Beck had been pleading with Fox News viewers to "vote" and "vote for America" to stop communists, Marxists, and Nazis from taking over the nation. On October 26 he deemed it no longer necessary to avoid using the words "vote Republican" and proceeded to invite numerous Republican political leaders and candidates to join him on the air and to ask them what they needed by way of directing viewers to aid Republican candidates. Beck had often exhorted his viewers to resist anyone telling them what to do, but now he was doing exactly that. For fervent adherents of the Tea Party, who identified with and trusted him more than any other public figure, that contradiction mattered not at all.

POLITICAL PAYOFF

in the

2010 MIDTERM ELECTIONS

THAT THE POLITICAL TIDE was turning in favor of Republicans, with or without the Tea Party, became evident in late 2009 with victories in governors' elections in New Jersey and Virginia. The faltering economy, Congress's messy handling of health insurance reform, and a reinvigorated conservative reaction took its toll on Democratic candidates.

Tea Party Ascendant

In early 2010 a political earthquake rocked Massachusetts as the late Ted Kennedy's Senate seat fell in a special election to a Republican state senator, Scott Brown, who waged a populist campaign as clever as that of his Democratic opponent was hapless. Driving around the state in a 2005 pickup truck with two hundred thousand miles on it, the handsome Brown, who as a young man had once posed in the buff for *Cosmopolitan* ("you couldn't see anything"), declared that the post he sought was not "the Kennedy seat" but "the People's seat." Meanwhile, his Democratic opponent, Martha Coakley, actually told the media that she did not see the point of standing in the cold outside Fenway Park to shake hands and solicit votes.

Though Brown attracted support from many Tea Partiers, he claimed not to be a Tea Party member, refused its endorsement, and failed to appear when the Tea Party Express rolled into Boston for a rally in April. In fact, during the following months Brown pursued a course independent of the Tea Party and the Republican leadership. By November one influential Tea Party blogger had put Brown on the Tea Party's "hit list" for 2012, and after more centrist moves on Brown's part Judson Phillips, the leader of Tea Party Nation, referred to Brown, on April 1, 2011, as "an April Fool's joke," charging that Brown "threw us [the Tea Party] under the bus."[1]

Brown's departures from Tea Party orthodoxy of course find their reasons in the electoral math of a normally Democratic and liberal state. But in the Republican primary season following the Massachusetts special election, some established candidates who did not adhere to the Tea Party line paid a high political price. FreedomWorks played a key role in those upsets.

The Washington-based organization began focusing on the 2010 elections early in January of that year, when it flew sixty local leaders (including Keli Carender) from twenty-four states to Washington, D.C., to plot electoral strategy. It targeted sixty-five congressional districts with incumbent Democrats FreedomWorks believed to be vulnerable and trained the activists, including some Tea Party Patriots, in campaign techniques, social media, opposition research, and media relations.

During the 2010 Republican primaries Tea Party–backed insurgent candidates enjoyed notable successes against party-endorsed rivals in Alaska, Colorado, Delaware, Florida,

Nevada, New York, South Carolina, and Utah. In the midterm elections, despite a few setbacks, the Tea Party helped the Republicans to a big victory, taking away Democrats' control of the House. The Republicans won sixty-three seats, forty-two of them going to candidates closely identified with the Tea Party. They enjoyed most success in heavily Republican areas but also performed well in some competitive districts.

The Republicans also captured several Senate seats, reducing the Democratic majority to 53. They won open seats in Pennsylvania, Illinois, Indiana, and North Dakota and defeated two Democratic incumbents, Blanche Lincoln in Arkansas and Russ Feingold in Wisconsin. Tea Party Express funding helped, while the senator most identified with the Tea Party, Jim "I'm Proud to Be Called Senator Tea Party" DeMint of South Carolina, used his PAC to pour millions into these races, to boost the chances of such Tea Party favorites as Rand Paul in Kentucky and Marco Rubio in Florida (who won), and Sharron Angle in Nevada and Christine O'Donnell in Delaware (who lost).

The 2010 outcome resulted in large part because independent voters swung away from the Democrats. But variable turnouts among demographic groups also counted heavily: who voted and who stayed away. The large numbers of young voters, Hispanics, and African Americans who turned out in 2008 to elect Obama disappeared in 2010. To compare just two sectors: in 2008 the 18-to-29 age group constituted 18 percent of the electorate, and the 65-and-over cohort 16 percent. In 2010 those percentages were 11 percent for the young and 23 percent for senior citizens.

Similarly, evangelical voters, whose support for Republicans and Bush had declined in 2006 and 2008, turned out in force. They made up 41 percent of the electorate, and 86 percent of them voted Republican. By 2011 the influence of the Religious Right had become associated in a major way with the Tea Party, although some Tea Party activists remained conflicted on this score.

They could as well have felt some ambivalence about the political action committees that pumped unprecedented millions of dollars into support of Republican congressional, gubernatorial, and state legislative candidates. The funding sources included FreedomWorks and the Tea Party Express, of course, but also two PACs organized by Republican strategist and Bush advisor Karl Rove: American Crossroads and Crossroads GPS. These PACs, taking advantage of the U.S. Supreme Court's 2009 *Citizens United* decision, did not disclose their donors' identities. Nonpartisan and Democratic watchdog groups charged that Rove's PACs in particular were engaging in unethical if not illegal actions.

President Obama had objected to the *Citizens United* decision in part because it opened the door to foreign money influencing U.S. elections. The 1907 Tillman Act made it illegal for "foreign nationals" to spend money in any way to influence U.S. elections. As the 2010 midterms approached Obama escalated that warning into a charge that the U.S. Chamber of Commerce could draw on funds from foreign companies in its high-spending campaign to defeat Democrats and elect Republicans. Earlier that year the Chamber of Commerce had successfully lobbied against the attempt of congressional Democrats to pass the Disclose Act, which would have required PACs to be transparent about their donors. Democratic accusations regarding the use of foreign funds rested, however, on the assumption that since money is fungible, dues paid to the Chamber of Commerce by foreign corporations might well be regarded as being used in our elections. Given the uncertainty involved, the website PolitiFact rated these accusations as "half true."[2]

Wherever the money boosting their campaigns came from, the eighty-seven new Republican members of Congress included a healthy number of mavericks and unconventional politicians. They said they were on a "mission" that allowed no compromise, damn the consequences, including risking reelection. For various reasons, but mainly to maintain ideological purity, nineteen of them bunked in their offices. Among them were a cotton farmer and gospel singer, a former intensive-care nurse, a former N.F.L. offensive lineman, a former reality TV star, and a former F.B.I. undercover agent whom mobsters had nicknamed "Mikey Suits." Fifty-two of them associated with the Tea Party caucus. Thirty-four of the eighty-seven had not held office before and called themselves "citizen politicians."[3]

The organizer of the Tea Party caucus, Michele Bachmann of Minnesota, already had established herself as a Tea Party darling for the verbal grenades she regularly threw at President Obama and her pithy handling of hot-button topics: homosexuality is a "dysfunction"; global warming is a "hoax"; the media should investigate "anti-Americans" in Congress; answering the census could get you thrown into an internment camp; and much more, all of which endeared her to the Tea Party.

The fifty-five-year-old Bachmann was born into a Democratic Lutheran family but gravitated to conservative views by way of pro-life advocacy. A person of enormous energy, the petite, attractive mother of five also took in for extended periods and helped to raise twenty-three foster children. Her entry into public life began with dissatisfaction with the public school experiences of her foster children. She had helped start a charter school whose Christian teachings aroused complaints and led to state intervention, so she ran for the local school board. By 2001 Bachmann had won election to the state senate, and two years later she seized on opposition to gay marriage as her signature issue. Christian conservatives rallied to her condemnation of homosexuality as sinful and reversible by prayer, and the issue became her path to election to Congress in 2006. By virtue of her red-meat right-wing rhetoric she soon became a media star and a formidable fundraiser. At the 2011 Conservative Political Action Conference (CPAC) Bachmann wowed the cheering throng of eleven thousand attendees by denouncing the "monstrosity of Obamacare . . . the crown jewel of socialism" and vowed to bend all her energies in Congress to defeating it. She also delivered, apart from the formal Republican speech, a separate Tea Party response to President Obama's 2011 State of the Union message. A Tea Party favorite, Bachmann decided to enter the Republican presidential primaries.[4]

Her pre-2010 election caucus included typical Republican congressional delegates, some of whom came from safely Republican (gerrymandered) districts and whose voting track record stamped them as highly conservative on fiscal and social issues. Yet Walter "Wally" Herger Jr. of Southern California, for example, had served in the House since 1987 and could not be described as far-right in his policy positions. A member of the Church of Jesus Christ of Latter-day Saints, Herger grew up on a large cattle ranch and plum farm owned by his family and had worked in his family's oil and gas exploration business. (Ties to energy industries are common among southern and western Republicans—as well as some Democrats.)

The House Tea Party caucus contained a strong Southern presence. As of 2011 nearly three-fourths of the House Tea Party caucus of sixty-four members hailed from southern or border states. Among the most attention-getting of this group was Joe Wilson of South Carolina, whose cry of "You lie!" during President Obama's first State of the Union speech in 2010 promptly attracted a flood of donations from die-hard conservatives and Obama-haters. In this vein too was Lynn Westmoreland of Georgia, who entered Congress in 2005 and rapidly became known for his support of business and the Religious Right. In 2006 he sponsored a bill that would have permitted the display of the Ten Commandments in public historical settings. When comedian Stephen Colbert asked the congressman to recite the commandments on his show, Westmoreland could come up with only three. More seriously, displaying the hard-core Southerners' antipathy to the civil rights movement, Westmoreland joined several other representatives who opposed renewal of provisions in the 1965 Voting Rights Act that require nine Southern states and certain counties to obtain federal permission before making changes to election laws. The group argued that the passage of time had made such requirements unnecessary. (An overwhelming bipartisan majority renewed the 1965 legislation for another twenty-five years.)

Before Joe Wilson interrupted the president's speech to Congress, Westmoreland in September 2008 had described Obama, then still the Democratic nominee, and his wife Michelle as "uppity," a mild enough adjective in isolation but not in relation to black Americans in the context of the historically segregated South. Westmoreland responded to the ensuing controversy by saying that he had "never heard that term used in a racially derogatory sense. It is important to note," he said, "that the dictionary definition of 'uppity' is 'affecting an air of inflated self-esteem—snobbish.'" In 2010 Westmoreland carried Georgia's 3rd Congressional District, the suburbs and country south of Atlanta, with 69.5 percent of the vote.

Coded racial language in the Republican Party and Southern politics in general is hardly a recent development. Since the 1960s, as white Southern voters changed their party loyalty from Democratic to Republican, racial appeals using race-neutral language have been a fixture of national and state and local political campaigns. Wilson and Westmoreland embody a nonracist but refined and implicitly racial posturing that employs symbols that refer to a continuing subtext of racial fears still entrenched in American politics—and one that predated the emergence of the Tea Party.

Among the dynamics of the 2010 midterms, however, race was not particularly salient except in that it may have heightened opposition to President Obama's policies. Among the newly elected Tea Party freshmen of 2011, cutting spending, repealing the new health legislation, saving tax cuts for the wealthy, reducing federal regulations on corporations, weakening the Environmental Protection Agency, and keeping the Republican leadership glued to a hard-right agenda seemed more on their minds than race. Of course the Tea Party caucus's determination to cut heavily into funds supporting the federal social safety net for the poor, elderly, and other disadvantaged citizens would harm lower-income African Americans (as well as Hispanic Americans) far more than middle-class whites.

Among the Tea Party's fresh faces in Congress was Allen West, the one winner among the thirty-two African American candidates the Republicans fielded. The first black person elected to Congress from Florida since 1876, West warmly welcomed the Tea Party's embrace and dismissed as absurd critics' suggestions that the movement was motivated by racism. West averred that he "scares" Democrats because he is "a black man who was brought up in the inner cities, career military, married going on twenty-two years, two beautiful daughters, and for whatever reason that really does scare them."[5]

A retired lieutenant colonel who served in Iraq, West left the military in 2004 after being disciplined and relieved of command for wrongfully coercing information from an Iraqi police officer. In 2008 West had challenged the incumbent Democrat, Ron Klein, who had won the historically

Republican southeast Florida coastal district in 2006 in that year's Democratic tide.

In his first campaign West had failed to attract significant money or support from national Republicans. But in 2010 as contributions poured in, his fundraising quadrupled, and he outraised Klein by a ratio of about three to two, receiving significant contributions from banking and finance interests. Endorsed by Sarah Palin and, in a YouTube video, by the popular football coach and Republican campaigner Lou Holtz, West benefited from low turnout and Tea Party excitement. With one-third of the 2008 electorate not bothering to vote West beat Klein by almost nine percentage points after having lost by ten points in 2008. Republicans regarded West, who once called President Obama "a low-level socialist agitator," as a rising star; he was named a keynote speaker at the February 2011 CPAC meeting and assumed a place alongside such established Tea Party stars as Bachmann and DeMint.

Other freshmen Republican members of the Tea Party caucus fit the pattern of traditional Republican conservatives more closely. Bill Flores of Texas, for example, upset a Democrat who had managed to survive for twenty years in a district heavily gerrymandered to favor Republicans. Flores, a former oil industry executive, received big campaign contributions from the gas companies and held predictable policy positions on economic and social issues. During the lame-duck session of Congress in 2010, when Tea Party groups urged new Republican delegates to come to a Tea Party orientation, Flores and the other freshmen held their own session, prompting jilted Tea Partiers to send the new members angry emails. On Fox News, Flores said he regarded those actions as "inappropriate."

The influx of highly conservative Republican lawmakers quickly registered an impact on both congressional leadership and policy. The House voted to repeal the health law passed by the Democrats; the bill was unlikely to survive the Senate and sure to face a presidential veto. It also slashed budgets for a variety of federal entities and programs, including the Environmental Protection Agency, the Corporation for Public Broadcasting, the National Endowment for the Arts, the National Aeronautics and Space Agency, and more. The seventy-three new Republican members kept calling for more drastic cuts, putting them at odds with the Republican congressional leadership.

The 2010 election and the Tea Party also led to the demise, at least temporarily, of the hallowed congressional practice known as "earmarks" (special appropriations for representatives' districts attached willy-nilly to larger bills). Tea Partiers continually denounced them and all such "pork barrel" spending. As a presidential candidate Obama also called for an end to earmarks, while his opponent Senator John McCain made them central to his campaign. But veteran representatives who had sent millions of dollars in projects back to their districts balked, as did the Tea Party caucus. In fact, during the lame-duck 2010 session of Congress, fifty-two members of the Tea Party caucus requested 764 earmarks on pet projects totaling over $1 billion in spending. Representative Denny Rehberg, a Republican from Montana, led all caucus members with earmark proposals to benefit his district, exceeding $100 million. But, true to their professions of purity, Bachmann and thirteen of her caucus colleagues made no requests at all.

When the new Congress assembled in 2011 pressure to ban earmarks came from inside and outside the Capitol alike. The Tea Party Patriots, now a national umbrella for many local groups, contacted its well over one hundred thousand online members to ask all congressional Republicans to ban earmarks. Within the House chamber, newly elected Tea Party members joined the chorus to ban them as well. Eventually both the Democrat-controlled Senate and the House banned earmarks for the next two years.

The emergence of the Tea Party resulted in the rebranding of the opposition to President Obama and the Democrats. The Republicans' own name had been tarnished by a four letter word: Bush. The anti-Bush fervor that swept the Democrats into control of Congress in 2006 and Obama into the White House in 2008 owed much to reaction to the Bush administration and Republican policies that had enlarged deficits and debt. In 2004, when Bush won reelection, 34 percent of Americans identified themselves as Republicans. By 2008 that figure had fallen to 28 percent, where it remained as late as 2010. The Tea Party's eruption into the political arena purified the Republican brand by directing public memory and media attention away from frustration and anger with the Bush administration. Indeed, the party of anger succeeded in channeling some of that reaction against the new Democratic administration, which inherited so many difficulties from the Bush-Cheney years.

Evangelicals and the Tea Party

Before there was the Tea Party as a key constituency of the Republican Party there were evangelicals and the Religious Right. A strong relationship exists between the two groups.

The population of the United States stands out as one of the most religious in the developed world, confounding the usual rules that underdevelopment and poverty indicate high levels of religious faith and vice versa. Secularism supposedly correlates with affluence, but not in the United States. Some 65 percent of Americans say that religion is important in their daily lives, compared to 30 percent in France, 27 percent in Great Britain, and 24 percent in Japan.

Religion understandably plays an important role in

American politics and, in recent decades, increasingly so in the Republican Party. The religiosity of much of the citizenry extends to what has been called the "Biblical Worldview" of the American people. According to polls taken between 1999 and 2004 by *Newsweek,* ABC, and CNN/*Time,* 55 percent of the nation's adults believe in the literal truth of the Bible. Among evangelical Protestants, the figure rises to 83 percent (as compared to 47 percent of non-evangelical Protestants and 45 percent of Catholics). Among the questions posed in the poll was "Will the world end in an Armageddon battle between Jesus Christ and the Antichrist?" Forty-five percent of all Christians think so, while 71 percent of evangelical Protestants agree.[6]

Fundamentalist or evangelical Protestants, many of them Southern Baptists, enjoy majority status in the American South and make up a prominent part of the Republican voting base. By 2004 white evangelicals had been a key Republican constituency for some time. More than three quarters of them voted to reelect President George W. Bush.[7] But during Bush's second term evangelicals became disillusioned with the president and the Republican Party. The war in Iraq was going badly, as civil war seemed to take over that suffering country. American combat casualties climbed much higher than they had been when Bush spoke in front of a "Mission Accomplished" banner in 2003; a number of incidents revealed the trumped-up case that had been made for the war; and in September 2005 the woeful administration handling of the devastation wrought by Hurricane Katrina sent the approval ratings of Bush and the Republican Congress plummeting among all religious groups.

Other events lowered evangelical morale in particular, as Republican members of Congress, most prominently House Majority Leader Tom DeLay, became embroiled in corruption scandals. In September 2006, just before the election, a Republican congressman from Florida, Mark Foley, re-signed after revelations that he had been trying to seduce teenage boys who had worked as congressional pages. In addition, David Kuo, a former White House aide who had worked on relationships with the Religious Right, left the Bush administration, disillusioned by the political calculation he encountered. Kuo's book, *Tempting Faith: An Inside Story of Right Seduction,* revealed that Bush's advisors routinely referred to members of their evangelical base as "nuts," "ridiculous," and "goofy."

As a result evangelical voting turnout during 2006 declined sharply, and in several states referenda favored by the Religious Right (for example, an extreme anti-abortion law in South Dakota) went down to defeat. Exit polls now showed that only 49 percent of evangelicals believed that President Bush's faith made him a better president.

In 2008 Barack Obama's presidential campaign sought to make inroads in the Republicans' once-reliable evangelical base. Enlisting moderate ministers and religious authors popular with younger evangelicals, the campaign organized hundreds of "American values house parties," while Obama visited ten Christian colleges in swing states. These efforts bore fruit.

While overall Obama claimed more evangelical voters by only 3 or 4 percentage points above Kerry's share in 2004, he doubled support among the 18-to-29 age group and gained similarly in the 30-to-44 cohort. A small but growing generational divide appeared among religious voters, with the younger groups less interested in same-sex marriage and more concerned about poverty, human rights, and especially the environment. Young evangelicals can now be found volunteering at homeless shelters for gay men, helping to combat AIDS, lobbying for action on climate change, and working for agencies that help relocate third-world refugees.[8]

In swing states Obama's gains were particularly impressive. In Colorado, one of the strongholds of evangelical America, home to dozens of megachurches and moral values organizations, Obama outperformed Kerry among evangelicals by ten points.[9]

The election of Obama, however, and the emergence of the Tea Party brought older, conservative evangelicals back to the Republican fold in force. Registering their highest turnout ever, evangelicals in the 2010 midterm elections constituted 29 percent of the electorate. Seventy-eight percent voted Republican; 52 percent said they supported the Tea Party.

Together evangelicals and Tea Party supporters made a powerful impact. By the following year, pollsters and pundits were asking if the Tea Party and the Religious Right amounted to the same thing.

THE TEA PARTY

and the

RELIGIOUS RIGHT

POLLS HAVE FOUND Tea Party supporters to be wealthier and better educated than the general public. Those who identify with the movement tend to be Republican, white, male, and older than forty-five years old. They hold policy positions more conservative than Republicans generally, especially on economic issues and in their attitude to President Obama.[1] Although angered by the Wall Street collapse of 2008, they are less likely to hold bankers, investors, and mortgage bundlers responsible for the damaged economy than politicians and the less affluent buyers of subprime mortgages.

Almost every analysis of the Tea Party's emergence mentions the recession, and one of its worst features for millions of Americans is unemployment, which stands at the highest level since the Great Depression of the 1930s. Unemployment does not seem to affect Tea Partiers much directly. One study found no relationship between joblessness and Tea Party membership.[2] Although this was not a survey of individuals but of cities, the finding suggests that the movement's grassroots are responding more to a general sense of economic insecurity and a gloomy future for the nation's economy. With millions unemployed, surely they know someone who has lost a job or is underemployed. A close look at the connection between the grassroots Tea Parties and the Religious Right, as well as the religious attitudes of many movement supporters, however, helps to illuminate why they view the causes of the recession and those responsible differently from many Americans.

Constitutional and Biblical Fundamentalism

Although their corporate allies urge Tea Partiers to play down social issues and concentrate on debt, spending, and economic issues, most of them are in fact far more conservative than the general public on abortion, same-sex marriage, and the other issues that preoccupy the Christian or Religious Right in the United States. Six in ten Tea Party supporters believe abortion should be illegal in all or most cases, compared with about four in ten of registered voters. They oppose same-sex marriage by two to one compared to a 42 percent to 49 percent split among all voters (and in contrast to rising support for same-sex marriage, particularly among younger adults). Surveys have found strong agreement on other issues between the Religious Right and the Tea Party.

The Religious Right's strong biblical fundamentalism, meaning belief in a literal interpretation of the Bible, finds a parallel in Tea Partiers' constitutional originalism. They maintain that for much of the twentieth century and especially during the New Deal, Congress exceeded its powers and violated the Constitution. The federal government, especially Congress, must be held to a strict interpretation of the Constitution. Like other Americans, however, Tea Party supporters are selective about which passages to ignore and which to revere.

Some observers argue that Tea Party evangelicals view the Constitution through a lens known as "Christian Reconstructionism." This fundamentalist movement preaches the rule of biblical law—the Bible contains the rules of right living—and also believes that God meant for secular government to possess only limited authority. Thus evangelical antistatism comes not just from a long tradition dating back to the American Revolution but also from biblical fundamentalism. Southern Baptist evangelicals, in particular, also stress that God ordained a patriarchal family, from which flow conservative evangelical positions on women, abortion, and other moral-cultural issues.[3]

What might be called the Christian-Biblical view of the U.S. Constitution has been around for some time. In 1992 Howard Phillips, a longtime conservative activist who had worked in several Republican administrations and left the party to run for president as a minor-party candidate, founded the Constitution Party as well as the Institute on the Constitution (IOTC). The institute offers a twelve-point course for Tea Party activists on the biblical basis of the Constitution. Phillips's goal has been "to restore American jurisprudence to its Biblical foundations and to limit the federal government to its Constitutional boundaries."

These beliefs found expression among some of the Tea Party candidates for congressional and state office during the 2010 elections. Christine O'Donnell, the Tea Party–affiliated Republican candidate for the U.S. Senate in Delaware, is perhaps best known for the media feeding frenzy she ignited with her admission that she had at one time dabbled in witchcraft. More significantly, however, O'Donnell embraced constitutional biblicalism. Speaking to two thousand attendees of the Values Voters Conference, a right-wing evangelical group, in September 2010, O'Donnell at first touched superficially on familiar conservative themes. At the end of her speech, however, O'Donnell said that her primary qualification for the Senate was an eight-day course on the Constitution she had taken in 2002, this from the candidate who, when asked in a debate which recent Supreme Court decisions she disagreed with, could not name a single one.

The Constitution, O'Donnell told the Values Voters audience, is not only a legal document but also a "covenant" based on "divine principles." For decades agents of "anti-Americanism" have trampled on it, but she saw it making a "comeback." Like the "chosen people of Israel" the Tea Party has rediscovered America's version of the "Hebrew Scriptures" and is leading the country into "a season of constitutional repentance."[4] O'Donnell, a flawed candidate about whom there emerged numerous issues involving personal responsibility and honesty, lost the general election by a landslide. But her views are not on the margins of the Tea Party. They reflect the finding of a 2010 American Values Survey that 55 percent of Tea Partiers—a higher proportion than among the Christian Right itself—believe that the United States "has always been and is currently a Christian nation."[5]

During 2011, polling of Tea Party supporters increasingly suggested a substantive overlap between the Tea Party and the Religious Right. Abundant evidence for that viewpoint emerged as state legislatures convened and newly empowered Tea Party representatives pushed forward agendas laden with objectives more cultural than economic. In Oklahoma and South Dakota anti-abortion bills took precedence, while in Montana legislators took on gay rights and considered a bill declaring global warming beneficial to Montana. Indiana passed a bill outlawing same-sex unions, and Utah approved a bill recognizing gold and silver as legal currency. It must be noted that proposals of offbeat laws are quite common when newly elected legislatures meet, whatever their politics. Norm Ornstein of the American Enterprise Institute wrote that some are introduced just to make a point, while others are offered by "lunatics" who really want them passed.[6]

Some that make it into law can be pretty serious, however, as in Texas, where Tea Party lawmakers approved a controversial bill requiring women to have a sonogram before an abortion. The previous November a member of the Republican executive committee circulated an email calling for the incumbent Republican house speaker, Joe Straus, a Jew, to be replaced by a "Christian conservative" since that was the character of the legislature that had been elected. Both of Straus's challengers denounced the email, and Straus overwhelmingly won reelection.

This episode suggests that while the Religious Right is a powerful force in the Tea Party, it is easy for the media (and liberal bloggers) to sensationalize its outer fringes. The possible whiff of anti-Semitism (denied by the official who circulated the Texas email) made more news than Straus's reelection. Yet other aspects of Tea Party ethnocentrism, even xenophobia, cannot be overlooked: in early 2011 Wyoming and Tennessee were among fourteen states that had banned or were considering banning sharia (Islamic) law, even though no one, anywhere, has yet proposed such a thing in the United States.

All of this fits with the not-surprising polls showing that religious evangelicals strongly support the Tea Party—five times as many are likely to support it as oppose it according to the Pew Research Center (44% vs. 8%). An October 2010 poll yielded similar results: nearly half (47%) of Americans who identified with the Tea Party also say that they are part of the Christian conservative movement.[7]

The white evangelical association with the Tea Party has apparently made an impression on those religious groups holding the least favorable attitudes to the movement. At one end of the spectrum are white evangelicals, who constitute a core of the Tea Party and Republican voters. At the other end are Jews, those unaffiliated with churches, and atheists and agnostics: 49, 42, and 67 percent of those groups, respectively, disagree with the Tea Party.

The substantial majorities of evangelicals who support the Tea Party are, however, not monolithic. Moreover, in February 2011 Pew Center analysts concluded that "support for the Tea Party is not synonymous with support for the religious right."[8]

Younger evangelicals have reacted negatively to the hateful images of the president seen at the early Tea Party rallies. They view Obama as a decent man and criticize vitriolic attacks on the president's character. He is, as they say, no Bill Clinton, and they believe he provides a positive role model for African American men. During 2008 evangelicals generally approved of Obama's willingness to discuss his faith and to discuss religion with them even while disagreeing about important issues such as choice for women and same-sex marriage. Reverend Susan Speakman of the Bethany Presbyterian Church in Bridgeville, Pennsylvania, changed her party affiliation from Republican to Democrat to vote in the state's primary. "What caught my attention early on," she said, "was his comment that we don't want red states and blue states, but we want to find reconciliation and rapprochement with folks."[9]

Sarah Palin has won the hearts of many Republicans and above all of Tea Party supporters. But her admirers do not generally seem to favor the idea of her running for president. Even during 2008 evangelical responses to John McCain's selection of her as his running mate revealed growing evangelical diversity, especially along generational lines.

Senator McCain selected Palin for a variety of reasons. Senator Hillary Clinton's candidacy for the Democratic presidential nomination had engaged the hopes of millions of women, and when she lost to Obama, McCain's camp calculated that disappointed Democratic and independent women would be drawn to the Republican ticket. This calculation emerged in part from media coverage of the Democratic campaign that may have exaggerated the potential for the transition from Clinton to McCain-Palin. Once Obama clinched the nomination before the Democratic convention and the uncertainty had gone out of the process, this faux media narrative of angry Clinton supporters became a way for reporters to manufacture tension and interest. In addition, Palin was expected to attack Obama and the Democrats on hot-button cultural issues, which she did from the moment she stepped onto the national stage with her dazzling acceptance speech.

But younger evangelicals wanted to get beyond that kind of campaigning and reacted negatively to the prospect of Palin heating up the culture wars. While most of them still fervently rejected abortion in any circumstance, they had moved on to issues of social justice and climate change. Even some older evangelicals regarded Palin as "culturally outside the mainstream of Evangelicalism." Palin's aggressive libertarianism and her culturally loaded rhetoric contributed to the gains Obama made among younger evangelicals.[10]

The Christian Right and Machismo

Guns and God have been conspicuous in American politics and show up loudly in the Tea Party movement alongside blunt, pugnacious talk. This is not a matter of overheated partisan rhetoric, which exists among all parties (and flowered in the opposition to President George W. Bush). But this heavily masculine style of rhetoric has historical roots in right-wing populist movements and in the language political leaders use when they strive to speak as one of the common people. There has been no lack of tough, machismo talk and posturing among the men and women of the Tea Parties, especially from the political candidates who have courted their votes.

Polls consistently show that more men than women, particularly older white men, are attracted to the Tea Party, but this fact can be misleading. Women have played key roles at the grassroots level and have been recruited by Freedom-Works to lobby for their pet causes. Women leaders of the Tea Party notably have used masculine, even military, rhetoric as much as their male counterparts. Sarah Palin introduced herself to the nation as a "hockey mom," a rough and ready woman of the outdoors who has shot wolves and moose. She refers to her loyal female followers as "Mama Grizzlies" and laces her speeches with military metaphors: "Don't Retreat, Reload!" During the 2010 election season her website featured a political map of the United States with gunsight crosshairs placed on the congressional districts of Democrats thought to be vulnerable.

Palin also infuses her language with "moral values" appeals, but perhaps no conservative political leader combines appeal to the religious right and a macho persona more than Texas governor Rick Perry. His tough talk attracted national attention in 2009 when he suggested that if the federal government kept up its profligate ways Texans might secede from the Union. He appropriately titled his 2010 book *Fed Up!*

Perry now has the distinction of being Texas's longest-serving governor and one who also set a record for the number of vetoes of legislative bills. One of them prevented a ban on executions of the mentally retarded. Meanwhile he has pushed into law many hard-line conservative policies, including the 2011 bill requiring a mandatory ultrasound before an abortion. He has not apologized for his associations with persons with extreme religious views or for the appearance at his 2007 inauguration of a friend and rock musician wearing a T-shirt with the Confederate flag.

Perry's embrace of conservative evangelicals rivals that of any Tea Party–inclined politician in the country. In 2005 he established the "Restoration Project" to increase the political involvement of fundamentalist ministers he dubbed "patriot pastors." Some of them, along with Tony Perkins of the Religious Right–affiliated Family Research Council, attended his signing of a gay marriage ban at a Christian school. Perry agrees with most Tea Party leaders that humans do not cause global warming and, not surprisingly, opposes regulation of greenhouse gases. In 2011, before he entered the race for the Republican presidential nomination, Perry was not as well known to Tea Party supporters as Palin or Michele Bachmann, but he had assiduously courted fundamentalist evangelicals while leaders of the Christian Right earnestly urged him to run for president. After he entered the race his willingness to support college tuition grants for the children of illegal immigrants encountered disapproval from many Tea Party supporters.[11]

Although lacking the nature-woman cachet of Palin, Bachmann, also a candidate for the Republican nomination, is just as well known for her unrestrained rhetoric. At a Tea Party rally she referred to the Obama administration as a "gangster government," and in making her formal announcement for president chose a town in Iowa that she believed (erroneously) had been the birthplace of Hollywood tough guy John Wayne. Bachmann knows that her red-hot choice of words has made her a prodigious fundraiser and a grassroots icon.

In the 2010 U.S. Senate Race in Nevada, Sharron Angle, the Tea Party candidate seeking to unseat Senate majority leader Harry Reid, provided additional evidence that the macho political persona is gender-neutral. Her challenge to Reid—that he should "man up" politically—attracted national attention, as did her warning that if the present government became tyrannical, it might be necessary to exercise "our Second Amendment rights."

Perhaps the toughest, rudest talk in the country from a

Tea Party–backed politician has emerged, surprisingly, in Maine, a state known for moderation and civility in politics. Current governor Paul LePage won election in a three-way race, also common in the Pine Tree State, after emerging from a crowded field in the Republican primary. He grew up in poverty and abuse, and his first language is French. At age eleven, after a beating from his father that put him in the hospital, LePage, the oldest of eighteen children, ran away from home and lived on the streets. He eventually went to college and business school and established a successful discount chain. Elected mayor of Waterville, a town of about sixteen thousand with a strong Franco-American heritage, LePage never bothered to polish his confrontational, intimidating political style.

A populist who shoots from the hip, LePage while running for governor threatened to "punch out" a reporter asking unwelcome questions—neither the first nor the last time he issued that threat—and during his campaign told a group of fishermen that if elected he might become known for telling President Obama "to go to hell." In January 2011 in response to NAACP complaints that he refused to attend the Martin Luther King Jr. Day commemoration (as Maine governors had in the past), he advised the group to "kiss my butt." Speaking to a group of business leaders, LePage called the NAACP a "special interest group," sparking outrage within Maine and nationally. Yet as mayor of Waterville, LePage had attended several similar Martin Luther King Day events, and over the weekend following his remarks changed his plans and showed up at an NAACP breakfast honoring King, though he did not address the audience.

LePage is the complete anti-politician who avoids tact and discretion like a disease. And many Mainers, who otherwise shun political extremes but value independence of party and politics, adore his performances (and the full context of his dustup with the NAACP suggests that they are indeed perfor-mances). He gives "straight answers" and lets the chips (and collateral damage) fall where they may. He may wear a suit but is no "slick suited politician."

The extent of LePage's pro-business assault on workplace and environmental regulations and social services has been breathtaking. After ending Maine's status as a sanctuary for illegal immigrants with an executive order, he pushed the big-gest business-oriented tax cuts in the state's history through the Republican legislature. His targets for free market "re-form" included child labor laws, public pension benefits, and the state's Medicaid system and minimum wage law. He suc-ceeded in getting repeal of Maine's thirty-year-old practice of allowing same-day voter registration along with a new photo ID requirement at the polls (later repealed by referendum). And his extreme Tea Party agenda ran into opposition even from Republican legislators, particularly in relation to the environment. Mainers care about their forests, lakes, rivers, and coastline. LePage has not appealed to evangelicals, but his aggressive style has played well with Tea Party supporters.

Unlike other Republican governors who have pursued hard-right agendas and seen their approval ratings plummet, LePage after six months won an approval rating of 43 percent (he was elected with 38 percent of the vote; the second-place finisher got 37 percent). Not surprisingly, LePage's approval rating among men was ten points higher than among women, with 52 percent of women disapproving.[12]

In contrast, Tim Pawlenty, former governor of Minne-sota and a recent candidate for the Republican presidential nomination, has a reputation for being understated. But at times, realizing the need to appeal to his party's Tea Party and conservative base, he too has taken on a Clint Eastwood persona. Addressing the Republican CPAC conference in 2010 Pawlenty invoked the dramatic encounter between

Tiger Woods and his wife the night she discovered his affairs. Pawlenty recalled that as Woods left their driveway his wife smashed the rear window of his vehicle with a golf club. Pawlenty exhorted his audience: "She said 'I've had enough, no more.' I think we should take a page out of her playbook and take a nine iron and smash the windows of big government."[13]

But guns rather than golf clubs tended to be seen at early Tea Party rallies, and movement supporters more than other Americans want to see gun laws further relaxed. A Republican Tea Party–backed candidate for Congress in Arizona, a former Marine, appeared on his website and at fundraisers holding a loaded M16 and urged his supporters to come "shoot one with him" for victory. While many opponents of the Tea Party own guns (as do many Democrats), the CBS/*Times* poll of 2010 found that 58 percent of Tea Partiers have a gun in the household.

In the kaleidoscope of American religion there exist many traditions of Christian masculinity that have proliferated in our own time. Hits on the Google search for "Biblical Manhood," for example, average 6,600 a month. It is not surprising that hyper-masculine performances delight many Tea Party supporters.

THE TEA PARTY

and

BIG BUSINESS

THE TEA PARTIERS DISLIKE big government and spending more than anything else, but some have a reputation for hostility to big business. Grassroots activists have often expressed criticisms of corporate wrongdoing that could just as easily have emanated from liberals. Yet public opinion surveys indicate that Tea Party supporters, much more than other Americans, are unconcerned about corporate malfeasance or government favors to companies (otherwise known as corporate welfare), mainly in the form of low taxes and federal subsidies. In this respect the identifying characteristics of the Tea Party reflect the views of many conservative Republicans. While various Tea Party groups and activists have often vented criticism of Wall Street, banks, and corporations, in general Tea Parties must be described as not hostile but rather as ambivalent or favorable toward big business.

Libertarian Fundamentalism versus Christian Fundamentalism

Attitudes toward income and wealth inequality in the United States also set apart Tea Party identifiers from the rest of the populace. Since the 1970s economic inequality has been growing in the land of opportunity; since at least the 1990s commentary on and awareness of this development has been widespread. Some groups are less equal than others, particularly African Americans and Hispanics, whose perception of themselves as "have nots" has grown sharply.

Income and wealth inequality now compare to the same levels that prevailed in the 1920s before the onset of the Great Depression. Many economists believe that today's concentration of wealth in the top 5 percent of the population contributed to the economic collapse of 2008.

In 2010 the Economist Intelligence Unit compiled a "Democracy Index" along with an "Income Inequality Index" for thirty-three developed nations. The United States compared fairly well to other countries on an index of "Global Wellbeing" (based on Gallup polls) and ranked in the top group, although behind ten other countries, including Austria, Canada, Norway, and the Netherlands. It also scored well on "level of democracy," though below fourteen others (Germany, Switzerland, New Zealand, and Denmark, to name a few).[1]

But the United States ranked among the worst in income inequality, food insecurity, and life expectancy at birth. The most stunning differential appeared in the stratospheric lead of the United States over other nations in prison population—surely an index related to economic inequality.

So what do Tea Partiers think about the fact that the United States has more inequality than, say, Pakistan? Although majorities of Americans believe that increasing economic inequality is a serious problem for the country (62% do), only 42 percent of Tea Party supporters agree, while 41 percent say it is "not that big a problem."

Underlying these numbers is the connection between evangelical and fundamentalist Christians in the Tea Party and their attitudes to capitalism and an unregulated free market. According to a 2011 survey, many Americans believe that

Christian values are in conflict with capitalism (44%) and the free market (36%), but among Tea Party supporters a higher figure than for any other group (56%) believes capitalism to be consistent with Christian values.[2]

Tea Party members also diverge from the majority on the issue of the wealthy paying more taxes than the middle class or the less affluent. Two thirds (66%) of citizens agree that wealthier Americans should pay more in taxes—75 percent of Democrats along with 58 percent of Republicans. Tea Partiers, however, are divided on taxes on the rich, 49 percent agreeing and 50 percent believing the wealthy should not pay more. Again the Tea Party religious factor comes into play. Majorities of all religious groups think the wealthy should be taxed more, but white evangelical Protestants are divided in about the same proportion as the Tea Party: 50 percent agree, 49 percent disagree.

When asked at a November 2010 Tea Party Patriots press conference about corporations that paid no taxes, a prominent official of the group, Mark Meckler, gave a reply suggesting indifference: "We've been suggesting a corporate tax holiday to allow these companies to come in and create jobs." When asked about financial regulation of Wall Street, he was similarly vague but said that it is "one of the things we're going to add to our list of topics."[3]

Revealing too were Tea Party reactions to an April 18, 2011, "Tax Day: Make Them Pay" protest organized by a coalition led by MoveOn.org, labor unions, Common Cause, Greenpeace, and liberal citizen action committees. The "Them" at issue were corporations and banks, such as Bank of America, that had paid no taxes for the previous two years, and General Electric, scheduled to pay none in 2011. In forty cities across the country from Florida to California small groups of protesters picketed outside banks and corporate headquarters demanding that profit-making businesses pay their share.

Sixty people showed up in Boca Raton, Florida, and chanted "Hey, hey, ho, ho, corporate deadbeats have got to go."

One hundred members of the Westchester-Putnam Working Families Party and labor unionists gathered at the U.S. Post Office in suburban White Plains, New York, to denounce twelve large corporations they dubbed "The Deadbeat Dozen." A forty-nine-year-old union business agent and Air Force veteran sounded much like a Tea Partier when he said, "I am angry as hell. Veterans are going to suffer $2 million worth of cuts and the government gives tax breaks to these corporations? Veterans are going to come home after fighting three wars and have no jobs."[4]

That same week Tea Party rallies, with larger numbers in attendance (though much lower than the crowds of 2009), also took place across the country. To the extent that Tea Party spokespersons and activists acknowledged calls on corporations to pay a fair share of taxes, they expressed no agreement or sympathy with the goal of "making them pay." Some said flatly that corporations need not pay taxes, since corporations create jobs.

In early 2011 newly elected Republican governor of Wisconsin Scott Walker threw the state into turmoil when he proposed stripping public employee unions of collective bargaining rights. He argued that the change was necessary to balance the state budget in tough economic times. Teachers, nurses, sanitation workers, and others—supported by police and firemen whose unions were not affected by Walker's initial proposal—mounted continuous protests at the state capital, Madison, involving thousands of people. David and Charles Koch have extensive industries in Wisconsin, contributed to Walker's campaign, and backed his effort to eliminate union bargaining rights. Indeed, included in the union-busting legislation was a provision giving the governor the discretion to sell off some of the state's publicly owned utilities.

On February 19 as throngs gathered again after several consecutive days of massive outpourings against Walker's plan, Koch operatives bused in dozens of Tea Party counter-protesters. A *Huffington Post* reporter mingling with the Walker loyalists told them that, according to the Wisconsin Department of Revenue, two-thirds of corporations in the state paid no taxes at all. Maybe businesses could help with the state's need for funds? Those questioned, unaware of that circumstance, merely commented that unions constituted a bigger problem. "Corporations should pay no taxes at all," said one, a professed libertarian. "That's a terrible idea." Another engaged in denial: "No, they pay their taxes. They pay their taxes."

Corporate astroturf groups that provide funds, training, and infrastructure for grassroots networks diverge in their primary goals from those sought by a large portion of Tea Party activists, particularly those who also make up a significant part of the Christian political right. The astroturf donors strongly prefer that the Tea Party networks avoid social and moral issues, urging them to concentrate on the pro-corporate agenda of lowering or eliminating taxes and regulations on pollution.

Corporate libertarians believe that hot-button social issues—the right to life, same-sex marriage, immigration, school prayer, religious displays in public places, and so forth—are at best distractions and at worst provocations that will alienate independent and moderate voters. This reflects in part a longstanding division in the Republican Party between "country-club Republicans," who tend to be moderate on social issues, and middle- and working-class "values voters" more concerned with moral issues.

FreedomWorks, a leading proponent of corporate libertarianism, is the offspring of Americans for Prosperity. AFP emerged in 2003 as a successor to Citizens for a Sound

Economy, created and funded by the Koch Family Foundation, and continued its multi-pronged campaigns to weaken labor unions, oppose health care reform and stimulus spending, and stymie efforts to make industries accountable for the pollution they create. Between 2000 and 2009 Koch Industries dramatically increased the amount it spent directly lobbying Congress and state legislatures, spending, for example, $857,000 in 2004 and $20 million in 2008.

The company's diversified enterprises proliferate from its core businesses of refining and distributing oil. The privately owned conglomerate's products include chemicals, minerals, fertilizers, pulp and paper, chemical technology equipment, and livestock. With interests in sixty countries and almost every state the company has fifty thousand employees in the United States and twenty thousand abroad. In 2008 *Forbes* rated it the second-largest privately owned company in the United States, with an annual revenue of $98 billion. In recent years government agencies have often fined the company for environmental damage (as well as for stealing oil from government and Indian lands), and in 2010 it ranked tenth on the list of top air polluters in the country. The only men in America richer than the Kochs are Bill Gates, Warren Buffett, and Larry Ellison.

For decades the Koch brothers operated under the radar, funding astroturf lobbying fronts, right-wing think tanks, books, magazines, and what must candidly be called propaganda efforts to advance a libertarian vision that relentlessly promotes their own economic interests. They have poured millions of dollars into efforts to deny climate change, to oppose laws to reduce carbon emissions, and to keep regulation of pollution lax. Recently, they have put their resources into lobbying against Wall Street regulation and net neutrality, an internet ground rule opposed by broadband suppliers who want to charge for different levels of service. They have contributed millions to the campaigns of conservative politicians at the national and state levels, mostly Republicans and, recently, Tea Party candidates. From 2006 to 2009 they spent $37.9 million lobbying Congress and state legislatures on oil and energy issues. A complete account of their dozens of political activities and libertarian ideological campaigns could easily fill a book, which would begin with the story of their father, who founded the company in 1927 and who in the 1950s was an original member of the far-right John Birch Society.

The Kochs' relative invisibility as political activists and ideological warriors came to an end, however, with an investigative essay by Jane Mayer in the *New Yorker* issue of August 30, 2010. "Indeed," wrote Mayer, "the brothers have funded opposition campaigns against so many Obama Administration policies—from health-care reform to the economic-stimulus program—that, in political circles, their ideological network is known as the Kochtopus." The article immediately attracted enormous attention from other media, and the brothers have become a favorite target for liberal critics.

The ties of the Kochs and AFP to the Tea Party have been well documented. After recounting denials of Koch involvement by company spokespersons and David Koch himself, Mayer provided ample illustrations of how AFP and the Kochs had "worked closely with the Tea Party since the movement's inception." In April 2009, AFP's thirty-four national office employees and thirty-five state-level employees worked hand in glove with the Tea Party to promote the Tax Day protests.

In August the organization spent several million dollars to fund "Hands Off My Health Care" bus tours of Tea Party activists to attend and disrupt the town hall meetings at which congressmen were attempting to discuss the new health care legislation. Thus, some of the angry protesters at those town hall meetings did not actually reside in those districts. A FreedomWorks organizer reportedly circulated a memo to trainees for the movable protest: "You need to rock-the-boat early in the Rep's presentation."

FreedomWorks and its president Dick Armey claim to be authentic representatives of the Tea Party. Armey served in Congress for eighteen years and after 2000 became a lobbyist for corporations with a salary of three quarters of a million dollars, making him not exactly a man of the people. But the Texan cultivates a folksy style, complete with Stetson hat and pithy aphorisms that accompany his transformation from Washington insider to populist tribune.

FreedomWorks spent $500,000 boosting the September 12, 2009, Taxpayer March on Washington. Its staff of twenty in Washington provided training seminars and other support to Tea Party groups involved in protests throughout 2009 and 2010. FreedomWorks improved communication among the Tea Parties by setting up a weekly conference call with activists across the country. Its staff also managed the listserv of the Tea Party Patriots, who often proclaim their distance from astroturf corporate money. But talking points and speakers for the Tea Party Patriots are frequently arranged by Americans for Prosperity and other political operatives on the Koch payroll.

FreedomWorks training draws heavily on imitating liberal pressure groups such as MoveOn.org and urges Tea Party activists to read the writings of Saul Alinsky, a hero to many progressives who influenced community organizing of the poor and other disadvantaged groups as early as the 1950s. It preaches the gospel of "imitate the enemy."

On several occasions David Koch has denied that he or his brother Charles have been involved with the Tea Party. Yet there is an internet video of an October 2010 AFP meeting with a smiling David Koch himself at a podium listening to reports from Tea Party officials on their activities and showing his appreciation by applauding.

Several other organizations funded by right-wing corporate money have cooperated with and sustained grassroots activities, including Americans for Limited Government, founded by Republican senator Tom Coburn from Oklahoma. Its leader is now a libertarian real estate magnate, Howard Rich, a Koch ally who has also poured millions of dollars over the past thirty years to limit government and promote an extreme free market ideology. Americans for Limited Government developed the database for the April 15, 2009, Tax Day rallies, and its thirty employees are supported primarily by funds from three large donors.

The Kochs are hardly alone as generous donors to right-wing think tanks, astroturf organizations, political campaigns, and Tea Party activities. Other prominent sponsors include the Coors beer family; the Waltons of Walmart; the Olin Foundation (one of the pioneers in creating a climate hostile to taxes, government, and all things progressive); Richard Mellon Scaife, banker, publisher, and heir to the Mellon fortune; Rupert Murdoch of News Corporation; and Phillip Morris and ExxonMobil. Scaife, it should be noted, became well known in the 1990s when he funded any and all efforts to find damaging material on Bill Clinton's business dealings or personal life.

These corporate interests also pay lobbyists, of course, who work the halls of Congress and state legislatures, directly promoting laws or opposing regulations in a way that enhances their clients' economic interests. In some instances, however, business lobbyists, claiming to be speaking on behalf of the Tea Party, appropriate the label and engage in blatant astroturfing on behalf of corporate clients. The Institute for Liberty describes itself as an "advocacy organization dedicated to combating the petty tyrannies of government, especially the impact of an ever-expanding regulatory state on small business." In the fall of 2010 the Institute for Liberty took up the cause of a huge Indonesian paper company to allow it to sell its products in the United States without paying tariffs (tariffs are "tyrannies," apparently). The group's president, Andrew Langer, went down to Long Wharf in Boston with a copy of the Declaration of Independence and compared a proposed federal tariff on paper from Asia to the British oppression of the 1770s.

This event coincided with a public relations campaign launched by the company involved, Asia Pulp and Paper. Langer insisted that the Institute for Liberty had not taken money from the company, though it was possible, he said, that Asia Pulp and Paper had paid others who then contributed to the institute. AP & P's lobbying came in response to demands by U.S. paper companies and their unions who requested tariffs on AP & P's imports because of unfair trade practices by Indonesia and China who were subsidizing AP & P's products. Greenpeace has also criticized Asian logging practices, and several big retailers have stopped selling AP & P's products. Langer insisted that his efforts to oppose tariffs on Asian paper have nothing to do with AP & P. Even so, three days after a company-employed lobbying firm issued a report attacking Greenpeace and labor unions, Langer released his own report echoing the same themes.

Could the ironies involved here be more striking? The Tea Party has a reputation—partly deserved—for "hating" big business, and in this case "big" meant a foreign corporation that was presumably undercutting American businesses. A majority of Tea Party supporters are opposed to or deeply skeptical of free trade.

But the Tea Party was nothing short of a godsend for the Institute for Liberty. Well before the advent of the Tea Party movement, Langer opposed net neutrality. By 2009 Langer had increased the visibility of net neutrality as a political issue, framing it as an instance of government tyranny. So out came signs at Tea Party rallies opposed to net neutrality. Whether those carrying the signs were people paid by Langer or genuine Tea Party supporters is not known.

The Institute for Liberty joined Americans for Prosperity and FreedomWorks in the raucous protests against the Democrats' health care reform. "A donor gave us some money [resulting in one million dollars' worth of advertising]," said Langer, "and we went out on the ground in five states in the space of like six weeks."

During 2010 the Institute for Liberty cooperated with another astroturf group on behalf of agribusiness behemoth Monsanto to relax federal regulation of its pesticide-resistant alfalfa. What Langer called a "grassroots method" framed "as a dairy issue and access to affordable food" succeeded. Langer boosted the cause by filing a petition with the Department of Agriculture containing 8,052 comments collected by telephone. But the comments were identical, and a random sample of fifty names by the *New York Times* found that three people were dead at the time that their names were used, and one respondent recalled a phone caller who had asked only if the affordability of food was important to him.[5]

Other efforts to profit directly from the Tea Party phenomenon involved a highly publicized convention in early 2010 in Nashville, Tennessee, under the rubric of Tea Party Nation. Tea Party Nation began as a social networking website in 2009, a kind of Facebook for scattered Tea Party groups. It is also a for-profit business owned by Judson and Sherry Phillips, who charged a $549 admission fee, which is more than twice the cost of most conventions. The additional $9.95 fee plus expenses for airfare and hotel annoyed some Tea Party groups as well.

Keynote speaker Sarah Palin nevertheless attracted a crowd, along with Michele Bachmann and other Tea Party stars—but Palin's reputed fee of $100,000 combined with the for-profit venue caused several groups to drop out. Some worried about the Republican National Committee "hijacking" the Tea Party, while Erick Erickson, a conservative blogger, wrote that the cost levied by a for-profit entity "sounds as credible as an email from Nigeria promising me a million bucks if I fork over my bank account number."

Erickson thereby missed the opportunity offered by the "Silver Sponsor" of the convention, TeaPartyEmporium. com, to buy bejeweled tea bags. Priced at only $89.99 each and available in tiger eye, bloodstone, mother-of-pearl, and onyx, the jewelry was designed to "galvanize feelings felt by millions of Americans" opposed to "a government hell bent on the largest redistribution of wealth in history."[6]

Developing Strains in the Alliance

The complicated relationship between the Tea Party and big business goes beyond the predictable exploitation of the passionate by the self-interested. Tea Partiers supplied with technical help and infrastructure are not necessarily manipulated as much as they are practical, taking advantage of a relationship they regard as one of mutual benefit.

Besides, neither Koch Industries, Wal-Mart, and their allied free marketers nor the astroturf lobbying groups lined up with the Tea Parties represent all of big business, corporate America, or the multitude of the nation's small businesses. Indeed, the enterprises of many global corporations based in the United States clearly are in implicit conflict with Tea Party positions—such as its hostility to free trade, its economic nationalism, and its opposition to government involvement with business. Corporations that benefit from government programs and largesse cannot be comfortable with certain "pure" Tea Party demands. Of course many benefits corporations receive from the U.S. government are relatively hidden and escape public view, permitting firms to denounce "big government" while accepting corporate welfare.

Since President Barack Obama took office, FreedomWorks has complained about corporations that have endorsed administration policies. FreedomWorks has pointed angrily to PhRMA (Pharmaceutical Research and Manufacturers of America) and its backing of the health care legislation and to companies in the Climate Action Partnership that backed cap and trade efforts. Flush with victory in the 2010 midterm elections, Armey announced a campaign to boycott corporations that had cooperated with the government. FreedomWorks launched a wave of attacks, particularly on the CEO of General Electric, Jeffrey Immelt, calling him the "king of crony capitalism."

Immelt's offenses included accepting the necessity to move GE to "green energy" as well as Obama's January 2011 invitation to serve as his liaison to business. "For too long," said FreedomWorks executive director Matt Kibbe, presumably with a straight face, "corporate elites have lobbied to profit from the size and growth of government at the expense of hard-working Americans," a practice the finer points of which his colleague Armey might well inform him. Unmentioned went the rivalry between GE and Koch Industries in the energy field and the Kochs' fierce opposition to any efforts to combat climate change.

FreedomWorks might have called attention to GE's profits of $14.2 billion worldwide and $5.1 billion stateside and its tax refund of $3.2 billion. Armey and Kibbe, however, as seasoned corporate lobbyists, know better than to raise issues redolent of corporate welfare or tax avoidance.

The U.S. Chamber of Commerce, as noted earlier, poured money into electing Republican and Tea Party congressional candidates in 2010. But the Chamber of Commerce is also nervous about various Tea Party proposals to eliminate the Federal Reserve, seal the nation's borders, and end investment in infrastructure. Tight controls on immigration, favored by most Tea Party grassroots networks, could deprive the agricultural industry of a major source of cheap labor.

During 2010 the Chamber of Commerce donated to the U.S. Senate campaigns of such Tea Party darlings as Rand Paul of Kentucky and Marco Rubio of Florida (both of whom won). But the Chamber was far more comfortable with the likes of former Hewlett-Packard CEO Carly Fiorina in California (who lost) and former U.S. Trade Representative Rob Portman in Ohio (who won). In South Carolina Nikki Haley, Tea Party phenomenon, and candidate for governor, polled well and seemed headed toward victory in the Republican primary (and eventually won the general election). A former small business owner holding orthodox Republican positions on taxes and regulation, Haley enjoyed enormous popularity with the Republican base. But South Carolina's Chamber of Commerce overwhelmingly decided not to endorse her because it feared her wholesale embrace of what it saw as the Tea Party's inflexibility.[7]

The divergence of interest between the U.S. Chamber of Commerce and congressional Tea Partiers emerged in early 2011 as the need to raise the national debt ceiling limit became entangled with Tea Party–allied legislators' demands for enormous spending cuts. The president and congressional Democrats said that the draconian cuts Republican freshmen legislators and the Tea Party caucus sought were unacceptable. Thus the prospect of a government default loomed unless Congress raised the debt limit by early August. Concerned about a default and a plunge in credit markets and the dollar's value, financial institutions and corporations began pressuring House Republicans to raise the debt limit. Since January 2011 the Chamber of Commerce, the National Association of Manufacturers, and the Financial Services

Forum had been quietly lobbying the recalcitrant lawmakers to compromise.

In May the Chamber of Commerce released a letter to Congress from a coalition of trade groups urging it to raise the debt limit. The Chamber's executive vice president for government affairs, R. Bruce Josten, said, "Failure to raise the debt limit by that time would create uncertainty and fear, and threaten the credit rating of the United States."[8]

Government officials such as Federal Reserve chair Ben Bernanke and Treasury Secretary Timothy Geithner as well as many economists joined conservative columnists warning of dire consequences in the event of default, but the Tea Party caucus stood firm. The Tea Parties' grassroots members could feel further confidence that their voices had been heard.[9]

As the deadline approached a large majority of the public, even a majority of Republicans, decided that it favored compromise. Even the Tea Party grassroots were split, with different polls showing half or slightly less than half of supporters opposed to compromise. Similar numbers actually favored both spending cuts and tax increases in the form of closed loopholes—for example removing lowered rates for oil companies currently raking in record profits. Yet the purists in the Tea Party electorate ultimately exerted influence out of proportion to their numbers, as the final deal included spending cuts and none of the revenue increases Obama sought through eliminating Bush's tax cuts for the wealthy and corporate tax loopholes.

In the end congressional Tea Party and Republican representatives, being even more inflexible than their base, ended up forcing Obama to agree to a debt limit deal wholly on their terms. The freshmen elected with Tea Party support repeatedly denied that a U.S. government default on its debt would be disastrous. They and many Tea Party supporters expressed the belief that default would not have "a serious impact."[10]

Tea Party intransigence surfaced also when the Republican House budget committee in May 2011 emerged with deep proposed cuts that the White House and Democrats pronounced unacceptable. But harsh as the cuts were, they were not deep enough for many Tea Party members. A group of activists quickly gathered at the National Press Club to vent their anger at House Speaker John Boehner and Budget Committee Chair Paul Ryan, the latter formerly held in high regard by Tea Party supporters. William Temple, chair of the Tea Party Founding Fathers, carrying a five-foot musket and flanked by a colleague dressed as George Washington, called Boehner "a surrendurist, if that's a word." Temple and others issued threats to run primary opponents against Republican freshmen who voted for Ryan's budget, threats that were endorsed by Michele Bachmann.[11]

Political fallout from Ryan's budget, which cut Medicare and proposed changing it to a voucher system, quickly appeared on the electoral landscape. Just a week before the debt ceiling vote, Republicans lost a special election in the strongly Republican 26th Congressional District in western New York. The seat became vacant when incumbent Republican Christopher Lee resigned after disclosures that he had sent shirtless photos of himself to a woman he had met on a website. In 2010, married and father of a small child, Lee had won a second term with 76 percent of the vote.

What might have been an easy win for any Republican became a toss-up because of two circumstances: a Tea Party candidate entered the race, splitting the conservative vote, and the House passed Ryan's overhaul of Medicare, permitting the Democratic candidate, Kathy Hochul, to campaign relentlessly on the "Republican attack on Medicare." Meanwhile, Jane Corwin, the mainstream Republican candidate, attracted support from Boehner and other national Republican leaders. Hochul, whose "every other word" in speeches and commercials was "Medicare," rode the backlash against Ryan's plans to change Medicare to a win with 47 percent of the vote. The Tea Party candidate took 9 percent. Liberal and conservative bloggers debated the meaning of the election, but congressional Democrats quickly stressed the importance of protecting Medicare.[12]

Democrats, unions, and seniors then took a page from the playbook of the Tea Party Express and Americans for Prosperity by showing up at some town hall meetings held by freshmen Republican House members and loudly protesting the Ryan budget's revamping of Medicare. The Democratic Congressional Campaign Committee targeted twenty districts newly won by Republicans that Obama had carried in 2008.

In Vancouver, Washington, first-term Republican representative Jaime Herrera Beutler kept calm as about half of a crowd of five hundred constituents badgered her with questions, boos, and catcalls. Her critics focused on Medicare and her vote for the Ryan budget, but she also heard an eruption of boos when a member of the audience sarcastically thanked her "for voting to defund NPR." Beutler replied that she enjoyed National Public Radio but "we're broke." Before the meeting about twenty protesters, some from Planned Parenthood, carried signs reading "Save Medicare: Tax the Rich." Outside a Chicago hotel where Paul Ryan was giving a speech protesters carried signs reading "Hands Off My Medicare," and some angry constituents also showed up at his town hall meeting in his strongly Republican district.

In Arizona freshman Republican Ben Quayle, son of former vice president Dan Quayle, also confronted angry senior citizens, as did newly elected representative Andy Harris in Maryland. Even Tea Party congressional caucus member Allen West of Florida, who is wildly popular with conservatives in his district, saw his town hall meeting dissolve into a shouting match between divided constituents.[13]

Tea Party congressmen, especially those who see themselves as "citizen politicians," are less susceptible to pressure from disaffected constituents or the Chamber of Commerce than career politicians. Even the outcome of the election in New York's 26th Congressional District may carry less weight with the Tea Party caucus.

What happens in their base, however, does matter a great deal, and in that sector resides the greatest potential for division within the various levels of the Tea Party—specifically between corporate lobbyists and the grassroots. In Pennsylvania a split has opened between the majority of the movement's grassroots, which prefers universal school choice, and a minority of activists pushing a school voucher bill that FreedomWorks convinced Republican state legislators to support. Many Tea Party groups in Pennsylvania oppose school vouchers, viewing them as a bailout of poor schools. FreedomWorks has hired two veteran Tea Party local activists to lobby the legislature, hoping that their support "would give the bill grass-roots credibility." The bill's legislative and grassroots opponents are now on the receiving end of media campaigns to discredit them. Kibbe of FreedomWorks called Tea Party opponents of school choice "bed-wetters."[14]

To what extent the Washington-based corporate agenda will create additional conflict with the Tea Party's grassroots remains to be seen. Tea Party activists are not exactly known for their docility; as a Tea Party sympathizer wrote in the conservative *National Review*: "The whole point of this movement is that these people hate being told what to do."[15]

FRUSTRATION

with

POLITICS *as* USUAL

In the United States in the 1990s "the angry voter" attracted much commentary from journalists and political scientists. Voter frustration with "politics as usual" found expression in many venues during that decade, most remarkably in the independent political movement led by Ross Perot and his 1992 third-party candidacy. But the political discontent of the 1990s differed in significant ways from turmoil that emerged during the presidency of Barack Obama.

Immediate Precursors of Tea Party Rebellion

Unconventional throughout his meteoric rise in public consciousness, Perot was probably the first to initiate a presidential campaign on a television talk show. On the February 20 edition of CNN's *Larry King Live* Perot responded to a leading question from King about running for president by saying he did not want to but might if "ordinary people" were to urge him to do so. Overnight a grassroots movement developed with radio talk shows deluged with callers beseeching Perot to run, and within days polls showed that he had significant support in the electorate.

By May Perot was an active candidate, leading both Bill Clinton and President George H. W. Bush in polls in Texas and California. The details of Perot's erratic campaign, his withdrawal in July, and his reentry in October need not be recounted here. Perot eventually attracted almost 20 million votes and close to 19 percent of the total, a remarkable result considering all the self-inflicted damage he did to his campaign and the hostility the television and print media showed his campaign after his peak in the polls in May.

Perot, the "billionaire populist," offered simple solutions to complex problems: he would erase the government's deficit by "looking under the hood." Presenting himself as a "folk hero" and speaking in clipped sentences with a down-home Texas twang, Perot promised to balance the federal budget, pursue economic nationalism, and practice "direct democracy" through "electronic town halls." His campaign innovations included staying home and using a television marketing strategy consisting of sixty-second spot infomercials and half-hour prime-time television segments in which he appeared with charts and graphs to lay out his diagnoses of the nation's problems and his solutions to fix them. He also relied on a grassroots network of devoted supporters, the core of which stretched back to his activism on behalf of Vietnam War POWs and MIAs in the 1980s, when he engaged in secret talks with the Vietnamese government. He clashed with professional political consultants during the early months of his campaign; in the last phase he used only loyal "political amateurs."

Although critical of "trickle-down economics" and in favor of increased taxes on the wealthy, Perot as presidential candidate directed most of his criticism at the nation's political elite and never took on the corporations that were downsizing and shipping jobs overseas. Riled-up voters responded to Perot's appeal to populist frustration with government and politics as usual. For them Perot's most attractive feature was that he was "not a politician." "What inspired and united Perot's supporters," according to historian Michael Kazin, "was the same 'mad as hell' conviction that had animated campaigners for George Wallace [but without the racial component], the last serious presidential candidate to run outside and against the two-party system."[1]

In 1993 Perot stayed in the spotlight as a leader of the opposition to the North American Free Trade Agreement, along with an odd coalition of unions and some conservatives. His warning that passage of a trade pact with Mexico would create "a giant sucking sound" of jobs headed southward delighted his supporters, but in a much-publicized debate with Vice President Al Gore, his own cross-border business activities undercut his position.

Perot primarily attracted independent voters and weak Democratic and Republican identifiers and not conservative Republicans or evangelical voters concerned with moral issues—a significant difference with the "mad as hell" citizens of 2009. Of the almost 20 million who voted for Perot, 53 percent were self-described moderates, quite a different profile from Tea Party members. Perot's "Reform Party" was very much a one-man show. It did not attract the Religious Right. Further, Perot showed no interest in issues important to the Christian Right, preferring not to discuss them. He was at odds with evangelicals on abortion, embracing a pro-choice position. Perot voters resembled the Religious Right and the Tea Party primarily in their being predominantly white.

Disaffection with "politics as usual" and professional politicians had surfaced in a major way before Perot's emergence, notably with a term-limits movement that began in 1990 when California voters decided by referendum to limit the number of terms for state legislators; many states already had term-limited governors, and the president of course may serve only two terms. From California the movement rolled into other states, and by early 1992 term-limits initiatives or bills had appeared in thirty-six states. By 1994 twenty-one states had approved term limits for state legislators by popular referenda, and eight had adopted term limits for their congressional delegates, with voters usually approving ballot measures by roughly 2-to-1 margins.

In May 1995, however, the Supreme Court ruled that only Congress and not state legislatures could set the terms of federal officials. By then the movement, powerful among elites, had lost some of its energy because of the Republican takeover of the House of Representatives in the midterm election of 1994. But while conservatives and Republicans had been closely associated with the movement, in several states Democrats and independents also promoted term limits.

Among the general public, in fact, conservatives were no more likely to support term-limiting initiatives than liberals or independents. Dissatisfaction with specific performances of Congress or state legislatures showed little relationship to the drive for term limits. Rather, this anti–professional politician movement shared with Perot supporters "frustration with the political process, manifest[ing] itself in an increasingly cynical electorate."[2]

In 1998 frustration with politics as usual and with familiar political candidates surfaced in spectacular form in Minnesota. In a three-way race for governor, nonpolitician Jesse Ventura defeated two established major party candidates, one of whom bore a surname well known to Minnesotans: Hubert H. "Skip" Humphrey III. Ventura ran an aggressive populist campaign on the Reform Party ticket, though he was not backed by Ross Perot, who kept his distance from a candidate who was arguably even more unorthodox than Ross Perot.

Ventura—a Slovak-American born James George Janos—

had served in the Navy's Underwater Demolition unit (he claimed to have been a Navy Seal; the UDT merged with the Seals after he left the service in 1973). He later launched a career as a professional wrestler with the name Jesse "The Body" Ventura. When his active wrestling career ended in 1984, he became a wrestling commentator, which led to various acting and television appearances. In his political debut in 1991 he ran for mayor of Brooklyn Park, a large suburb of Minneapolis–St. Paul, and defeated a twenty-five-year incumbent.

His campaign for governor stressed his military career, his plain-spoken machismo persona, and the slogan "Don't Vote for Politics as Usual." His fans' favorite campaign slogan was "A Vote for Jesse Ventura Is a Vote for Jesse Ventura." Spending far less than his opponents, he made extensive use of the internet, grassroots events, and offbeat television commercials. Selecting a female schoolteacher as his running mate, Ventura promised to cut taxes, reduce state government, and make public classroom sizes smaller. He even encouraged a public debate about legalizing prostitution, but most of all he proclaimed that he was not a politician and that as governor he would be the common man with common sense. He won the three-way contest with 37 percent of the vote, besting the much better-known Humphrey by three percentage points.

In his tenure as governor, Ventura's outspoken and unpredictable policy positions stamped him as a most uncommon officeholder. With Minnesota running a budget surplus, Ventura succeeded in getting rebate checks on the sales tax sent out to citizens during each of his four years in office. Having declared his intention not to seek a second term, he felt free to endorse a unicameral legislature, gay rights, same-sex marriage, and the medical use of marijuana. Expressing his support for gays serving openly in the military, Ventura joked in a radio interview that he would have gladly served alongside homosexuals in the Navy since they would have not provided any competition for women. Clearly, like Perot, Ventura did not appeal to evangelicals of the Religious Right. He too endorsed freedom of choice for women and vetoed a bill to require recitation of the Pledge of Allegiance in schools. Ventura's career demonstrated that frustration with politics as usual cut a wide swath through the contemporary American electorate.

In the 1990s, too, voters who could made heavy use of the initiative and referendum process. A legacy of the early-twentieth-century Progressive era (notably adopted in California), initiative, referendum, and recall gave citizens in certain states remarkable access to policymaking. During the decade activists put more than three hundred ballot initiatives on ballots across the country, averaging sixty in each general election. In November 1996 a record ninety-one initiatives appeared on state ballots for voter approval or rejection. Not all of these ballot propositions came from grassroots citizens caught up in a cause; rather, some originated with corporations and special interest groups that had paid large sums for signature collecting by hired workers. (One side benefit of this outpouring of "direct democracy": states with referenda experienced voter turnout rates 7 to 9 percentage points higher in midterm elections and 3 to 4.5 percentage points higher in presidential elections.) Despite the role of astroturf groups, most initiatives expressed a broader impulse to effect an end run around unresponsive legislatures and political stalling, thus sharing a kinship with Perot's candidacy and the Ventura ascension.[3]

Unlike the contemporary Tea Party, however, all of these populist eruptions cut across party and ideological lines and, as with the Perot phenomenon, were anchored close to the center of the American political spectrum. They embraced in their heterogeneity populisms of left, center, and right. The

Tea Party, in contrast, has emerged from the right wing, particularly among "staunch conservatives," while its grassroots echoes the anger, frustration, and cynicism with the politics as usual of the 1990s and after. The contemporary right-wing grassroots rebellion, however, differs strikingly from earlier mobilizations by enjoying a sometimes uneasy alliance with powerful astroturf groups and with Tea Party caucuses in Congress and state legislatures.

Libertarianism with Benefits

Libertarianism with benefits is a syndrome that refers to the libertarian limits of many supporters of the Tea Party, particularly of the elected officials and lobbyists professing Tea Party principles. The term points out that in many instances the professed desire to be free of government has its limits, especially with regard to one's personal well-being. It refers to Congressmen, governors, and other elected officials who loudly protest against big government and spending while stretching out their hands to receive government benefits for themselves as individuals or for their districts. The syndrome of libertarianism with benefits also describes the actions of corporate executives who fund astroturf campaigns against government programs and regulations while lobbying for tax credits and tacitly accepting corporate welfare. The political crown prince of this syndrome is Dr. Rand Paul, Kentucky's new Republican senator, an ophthalmologist and member of the four-person Senate Tea Party caucus. Son of the more consistent libertarian and maverick congressman Ron Paul, the younger man owed much of his electoral success in 2010 to the Tea Party—as well as to out-of-state donations from conservative PACs.

Paul campaigned against the Affordable Care Act and championed small government. He once said he regarded

Medicare, Medicaid, and Social Security as "technically" unconstitutional. During his general election campaign, however, the question of Paul's own medical practice arose. With about half of his patients depending on Medicare or Medicaid, Paul defended his receipt of government payments and predicted that if he refused to participate in the programs he would "penalize his older patients or his poor patients." Patients would ultimately pay a price because physician shortages would result. He also opposed pending cuts to Medicare that would affect payments to doctors. The conservative commentator David Frum opined that "Rand Paul's libertarianism stops where his pocketbook starts," but given Paul's practice in rural Kentucky his point about injury to his patients has some merit.

In Maryland a physician who ran for Congress and emphasized his opposition to "Obamacare," even though his conservative Democratic opponent had voted against the new health reform, indicated after the election his eagerness to benefit from a similar government program. Andy Harris, an anesthesiologist from the state's Eastern Shore, vaulted into the twenty-four-hour news cycle when he attended an orientation for freshmen representatives and discovered that he would have to wait twenty-eight days before his government-run and government-subsidized congressional health insurance would kick in. An alarmed Harris asked why it took so long and what he was supposed to do for twenty-eight days without health care. (The House and Senate system of health coverage could be described as a version of the "socialized medicine" Harris had denounced in his campaign.)

Harris was quoted as saying, "This is the only employer I've ever worked for where you don't get coverage the first day you are employed." Harris, who had worked at various hospitals, could, under the federal COBRA law, pay a premium to extend his current health insurance for a month.[4] Fox News, always ready to provide a forum for misunderstood Republicans, gave Harris air time to deny that he had pitched a "hissy fit" at the orientation.

In contrast to Harris, one new Tea Party representative opted out of Congress's health insurance and its pension plan. Elected in a Republican year in an Illinois district based in Chicago's affluent northern suburbs, Joe Walsh squeaked into office by less than three hundred votes. A Green Party candidate drew off close to 6,500 votes—many of which probably would have gone to incumbent Democrat Melissa Bean. The district, once a Republican bastion, had swung in recent decades to be more hospitable to a fiscally conservative Democrat like Bean, who, after winning election in 2004, had steadily increased her majorities in subsequent elections.

Walsh presented himself as a Tea Party candidate and ran hard against the Affordable Care Act and the Bush-Obama bailouts of banks and auto companies. He received little money from the national Republican campaign, a fact that may have inspired his post-election comment critical of Republicans and Washington politicians. Republicans, he said, provided "welfare for the rich and corporations at the expense of small business," while many politicians are addicted to power and perks "and want to be something, not do something." In refusing to accept government-run health care, Walsh called it too generous. He also opposed ethanol subsidies, courageous heresy in any corn-producing state.[5]

His opponent's campaign had revealed that Walsh had had some difficulty with unpaid debts, had lost his driver's license, and had been found guilty of driving without automobile insurance. But Walsh's principled refusal of congressional health care, along with his embrace of down-the-line conservative positions, endeared him to Tea Party supporters and other constituents.

While Joe Walsh embodies a Tea Party dream come true,

other legislators fall short of the movement's purist ideals. Anger against bailouts of Wall Street financial firms provided the fuel that stoked the rise of the Tea Party, but that did not prevent ten Tea Party–backed freshmen representatives appointed to the Financial Services Committee from accepting almost $600,000 in campaign contributions from banks and investors in the months after the 2010 election. Those legislators then joined in pushing Republican bills that would weaken many provisions of the Dodd-Frank financial reform law passed the previous summer. Representative Spencer Bachus of Mississippi, in Congress since 1993 and the incoming chair of the Financial Services Committee, made his priorities clear: "Washington and the regulators are there to serve the banks."[6]

Committee member and freshman Republican representative Nan Hayworth of New York said during her campaign that she was "proud to be a member" of the Tri-State Sons of Liberty. She promised voters that she would vote to repeal both health care reform and Wall Street regulation. In 2011 Hayworth advocated the "Burdensome Data Collection Relief Act," which would repeal Dodd-Frank's CEO pay-disclosure provision. Not surprisingly, Citigroup, Bank of America, and J. P. Morgan were among Hayworth's campaign donors.

Newly elected Republican Sean Duffy of Wisconsin, a handsome former television commentator and reality show star, introduced a bill that would make it easy to obstruct any actions by the new Consumer Financial Protection Bureau. When appointed to the House Financial Services Committee Duffy admitted that he "wasn't very familiar" with banking and insurance issues. Meanwhile, businesses affected by the committee had contributed heavily to his campaign and then helped raise his reelection funds to almost $250,000.

This largesse was no doubt welcomed by Duffy, who in late March 2011 attracted publicity on the subject of his congressional salary of $174,000. A constituent asked him if he thought that, given the economy, the figure might be too high. Should congressmen also make sacrifices? Duffy replied by lamenting that he was barely making ends meet—driving a used minivan, paying too much for health insurance, and struggling to pay his bills. The voter observed that Duffy's salary was more than three times his own; indeed, a congressional salary does amount to almost three times the median income in Wisconsin. Liberal bloggers had a field day with Duffy's response, but in his defense, Duffy lacked employment for some time before his election to Congress, has six children, and is one of the nineteen freshmen Republicans who are bunking in their Washington offices. His willingness to serve the needs of the financial industry suggests that whatever fallout lingers from his congressional pay remarks, his reelection campaign will be well funded.[7]

Most Tea Party–backed candidates declared that they shared their constituents' disapproval of lobbyists' influence and money in Washington. Kristi Noem of South Dakota not only decried the nefarious practices of lobbyists "throwing money at the feet of a member of Congress" but also made a campaign issue of incumbent Democratic representative Stephanie Herseth Sandlin's 2007 marriage to a lobbyist (and former congressman). After defeating the moderate Sandlin, who had voted against the health care law, Noem promptly hired a lobbyist as her chief of staff.[8]

Other newly elected Republican legislators hired lobbyists to run their offices, at least thirteen as of December 2010. By then dozens had held fundraisers to raise millions from lobbyists and other special interests.

Noem is not listed as a member of the House Tea Party caucus, but she is touted as a rising GOP star because of her youth (thirty-nine years old), good looks, and persona as a horse-riding rancher and hunter. Comparisons to Sarah Palin of course have abounded. She also has voted as a staunch conservative since entering Congress.

Her record also sports several inconsistencies as well as acceptance of the help big government can provide agricultural enterprise. Noem echoed the Tea Party cry for eliminating earmarks but defended continued federal funding for a South Dakota regional water system because it was a project that had "already been vetted" and "authorized for years." Along with nine other House members she also requested federal aid to fight pine beetle infestation in the Black Hills and opposed cuts in subsidies to ethanol pumps.

All representatives, of course, want to show that they are providing help to constituents. So too with other Tea Party freshmen in early 2011 who found themselves requesting President Obama to help flood-stricken residents of their districts. Noem, however, benefits personally from federal government aid. This self-described "rancher" also owns a 16.9 percent interest in Rakota Valley Farms, a large agricultural enterprise that leads all others in the state in acquiring federal subsidies. Between 1995 and 2008 Rakota received nearly $2.8 million in federal farm subsidies.[9]

But Noem is hardly the only antigovernment Republican congressperson to receive federal aid to agribusiness. Stephen Fincher won election in 2010 in a historically Democratic district in western Tennessee and joined the Tea Party caucus. Fincher is a managing partner of Fincher Farms, a family business that grows crops on 2,500 acres and has received $8.9 million in farm subsidies over the past decade.[10] First-time congresspersons Noem and Fincher thus take their place alongside such better-known small-government Republicans as Chuck Grassley, Sam Brownback, and Michele Bachmann, all of whom have also profited from farm subsidies. Bachmann enjoys an additional link to big government through her husband Marcus, a clinical psychologist who offers "quality Christian counseling" at his clinic in Lake Elmo, Minnesota. Since 2005 he has received $137,000 in Medicaid payments.

Members of the Tea Party caucus in Congress range widely in their willingness to use government programs. Cliff Stearns, a Florida Republican, has served in Congress since 1989. He joined the Tea Party caucus when Michele Bachmann organized it in 2009. Stearns's Tea Party credentials are impeccable. The conservative National Taxpayers Union has given him an "A" grade, and he has joined in recent Republican / Tea Party attacks on the Environmental Protection Agency (he also voted for a bill requiring an F.B.I. "terrorist check" for 9/11 first responders seeking compensation). Stearns loudly echoes the Tea Party complaint that federal spending has grown too fast. But during 2008 to 2010 Stearns requested no less than $85,810,000 for his district. He also took credit for the 2010 opening of a lithium ion battery factory in his state that relied on an Energy Department grant.[11]

When in January 2011 the newly elected Republican representatives gathered in Washington, libertarian billionaire David Koch, a "funding father" of the Tea Party and contributor to the campaigns of many of the freshmen delegates, showed up to invite them to a party celebrating the Republicans retaking the House. While sharing a similar antigovernment, antiregulatory, and antitax policy agenda with the Tea Party congressmen, David and his brother Charles also share a willingness to enjoy income derived from taxpayer-funded government programs when it suits them. They too exemplify libertarianism with benefits.

These advantages go well beyond the tax subsidies conferred on Koch Industries along with other oil- and gas-producing corporations. Koch Industries exploits other government programs, such as those provided by the United States Forestry Service to their timber logging company,

Georgia Pacific, and by a New Deal program that allows its Matador Cattle Company to profit from federal lands. The Kochs' pragmatism is best illustrated, however, by their application to participate in the Department of Health and Human Services' new Early Retiree Reinsurance Program. This five-billion-dollar program, established by the Affordable Care Act, helps employers maintain coverage for early retirees age fifty-five and older who are not yet eligible for Medicare. That would be the same program ("Obamacare") against which the Koch brothers launched an aggressive, vitriolic campaign managed by their astroturf creations FreedomWorks and Americans for Prosperity.[12]

In 2010 the Kochs also contributed heavily to Republican candidates for governor in several states. Republican governors associated with the Tea Party, true to the practice of libertarianism with benefits, have maintained a circumspect silence about the agricultural subsidies their states enjoy. Governor Rick Perry of Texas has claimed he was a Tea Partier before there was a Tea Party. Whatever the case, Texas leads all states in the amount of taxpayer-funded subsidies to agriculture, receiving $24.4 billion between 1995 and 2010 (libertarian congressman Ron Paul's district received $1.54 billion). Michigan's new Republican governor, Rick Snyder, launched a Tea Party–favored game plan similar to that pursued by Scott Walker in Wisconsin. Snyder's budget removed the Michigan Business Tax and added taxes for seniors and retirees, cut funds to education and welfare, and demanded concessions from state employees.

Meanwhile, Michigan ranks twenty-second among states in federal agricultural subsidies to the tune of $4.3 billion between 1995 and 2010. Wisconsin, with almost $6.3 billion received during the same fifteen-year period, ranks fifteenth. Three Republican state senators pushing Wisconsin's hard-right laws have interests in agricultural enterprises that received $300,000 since 1995. In most states these payments do not go to the great majority of small farmers. Eight out of ten dollars typically go to fewer than a hundred firms. Congressional districts of both Democrats and Republicans receive these subsidies, and members of both parties in state legislatures likewise benefit.[13]

These cases do not represent even the tip of the iceberg. According to the Catalog of Federal Domestic Assistance, 2,025 federal subsidy programs exist with beneficiaries of all sizes and political postures. Health and Human Services runs the most, with 383 programs, while Agriculture ranks second with 230.[14]

Tea Party freshmen also rapidly learned Washington's way of directing defense spending pork to their districts. Newly elected representatives loaded the huge defense appropriations bill with home district projects they excluded from the category of excessive spending—to the amount of over $500 billion by one estimate. Vicky Hartzler of Missouri in a close election knocked off seventeen-term incumbent Democrat Ike Skelton, running on a platform of tax cuts, spending cuts, opposition to same-sex marriage, and pro-life. She also called for ending earmarks but gained $20 million to improve bombers at Whiteman Air Force Base in her district. A member of the Tea Party caucus, Hartzler said she believed the moratorium on earmarks did not apply to defense spending.[15]

The inconsistency that Tea Party politicians and their corporate allies display toward the largesse of federal government programs is shared by many of their grassroots constituents. While Tea Party supporters brim with passion in calling for repeal of the Affordable Care Act (83% favor repeal), majorities of them would nevertheless keep certain popular provisions. The health law debate sharpened public awareness of private health insurance companies' denial of coverage to patients with preexisting conditions. An October

2010 Bloomberg poll found that 57 percent of Tea Party supporters would keep this part of the reform. Fifty-two percent would add more prescription drug benefits for Medicare users, and 53 percent would require states to set up plans for people with major health problems.[16]

Some Tea Partiers do find themselves in a dilemma when asked if they wish to discontinue Social Security or Medicare, programs from which many of them personally benefit. A *Wall Street Journal*/NBC News poll in early 2011 found that over 70 percent of Tea Partiers feared that Republican legislators would not cut enough spending. But by a nearly 2-to-1 margin, movement supporters responded that cuts to Social Security would be "unacceptable." One resolved this dilemma by saying, "I guess I want smaller government and my Social Security."[17]

THE TEA PARTY

and

AMERICAN
POLITICAL CULTURE

SO WHAT IS THE FUTURE of the Tea Party? There are perhaps as many predictions as there are interpretations of its character. Many Tea Party activists insist that they plan to stick around for a long time, pressuring both Democrats and especially Republicans to commit to lower (or no) taxes and huge spending cuts. They will persist in the fight for smaller government and debt reduction.

Most of the corporate astroturf lobbying and political fundraising organizations predated the Tea Party—some under different names—so they will not likely be closing up shop anytime soon. Indeed, they show every sign of magnifying their activities, with or without the Tea Party, in the 2012 elections.

Predictions and Assessments

A political scientist sympathetic to the Tea Party concluded shortly after the 2010 midterm elections that the grassroots' "chronic decentralization and lack of organization suggests it will not endure very long beyond the midterm." Too many party activists, he concluded, "dislike party politics and refused to combine their grassroots energies into a coordinated electoral effort." The astroturf groups did the fundraising and organizing, he observed, with the result being a "windfall" for the Republican Party, which was now likely to direct the political fortunes of the Tea Party.[1]

Other number crunchers pointed to the lack of Tea Party success in big cities and populous states. The Tea Party–backed candidate in New York's gubernatorial contest lost by twenty-seven points, while in New Jersey Republican Chris Christie won election but kept his distance from the Tea Party. New York City, Los Angeles, San Francisco, Atlanta, Chicago, Philadelphia, and other cities all proved inhospitable to the Tea Party.

For quite a different reason, Andrew Sullivan, the prominent conservative author, editor, and commentator, saw the Tea Party's career as likely to be brief. Recent polls had revealed Tea Party activists responding to questions about race differently depending on their perception of the race of the questioner—indicating, as shown by other polls, a lack of minimal sensitivity to minority groups. "One part of the Tea Party's appeal is its ethnic solidarity," he concluded, "wrapped in nostalgia, paranoia, and fear. It makes a powerful package. But a doomed one."[2]

Polling in the early months of 2011 did indicate that the Tea Party, however committed its passionate core, was losing popularity. Among "staunch conservatives," to be sure, who constituted 11 percent of registered voters, the party remained in favor, with 72 percent agreeing with it. But only 32 percent of a group the Pew Research Center labeled "Main Street Republicans" agreed with the Tea Party.

"Tea Party: Better Known, Less Popular," concluded the

Pew Center analysts. From March 2010 to April 2011 the percentage of adults agreeing with the Tea Party remained about the same. But during that time those disagreeing grew sharply, especially among Democrats and independents. As Democrats' awareness of the Tea Party increased, their disagreement with it rose dramatically, doubling from 24 to 51 percent. During the spring and summer of 2011 the unwillingness of Tea Party congressional representatives to compromise even with members of their own party drew criticism from moderate conservatives such as *New York Times* columnist David Brooks and fed unfavorable perceptions of the movement—which registered in opinion polls.[3]

Poll results vary, but it should be said of the Tea Party, to paraphrase Mark Twain, that reports of its death are greatly exaggerated. In any case they miss the significance of its impact. Washington's political agenda in the spring and summer of 2011 was dominated by the debate between Republicans and President Barack Obama (and Democrats) over how to reduce spending and the standoff over raising the debt ceiling. Under pressure from Republicans, who in turn have been pressured by the Tea Party and have the results of the 2010 elections firmly in mind, Obama proposed far more spending cuts in the federal budget than he and Democrats really believed to be wise policy. Congressional Republicans in all negotiations with the administration and Democrats manifest a Tea Party–induced inflexibility. The effect of the Tea Party on the Republican base has been enormous, even as the blurred lines between the movement and the Republican Party have persisted.[4]

Despite the blowback against the Ryan budget and its changes to Medicare and Medicaid, when the *New York Times* editorialized in mid-April that a "mania for budget cutting" has spread from the nation's capital to statehouses throughout the country, then the Tea Parties' success—whether grassroots or astroturf—becomes clear. Tea Party influence—or, in effect, the pronounced rightward shift of the Republican base that votes in primaries—has also shaped the policy positions of the field of early contenders for the Republican nomination.

Mitt Romney, the presumptive frontrunner and early leader in polls, as governor of Massachusetts had worked with Democrats to enact a state health insurance plan similar to the one ultimately adopted in the national legislation, including a mandate for the uninsured to buy insurance. Romney, who lacked support in 2008 among Republican evangelicals and the right wing of his party, found himself on the defensive as he geared up for 2012. He countered that what worked in Massachusetts should not replicated on the national level, that "Obamacare" was a bad version of the Massachusetts plan, and that each individual state, he said, should design its own health insurance. The drumbeat of criticism of the Affordable Care Act from right-wing media and from both the Tea Party astroturf and grassroots has created a vulnerability for Romney as he vies for the Republican nomination. His opponents eagerly attacked him on this issue, and Freedom-Works, amassing millions for the primaries and general election, declared its top goal for 2012 to "Stop Romney."[5]

The shift on climate change among the Tea Party base also entered into the Republican primary process. During the past five years belief that climate change or global warming results from human activity has declined among Republicans. Indeed public opinion shifted to disbelief even as scientific opinion became nearly unanimous—in the United States and in countries around the world—that humans do contribute significantly to climate change. But a media barrage of climate-change denial promulgated by fossil fuel interests has lowered public concern about climate change to a weak majority, particularly among independents and conservative Republicans.

The candidate most identified with the Tea Party, Michele

Bachmann, denies that humans cause climate change and maintains that carbon dioxide occurs "naturally." Meanwhile, Romney and candidates Tim Pawlenty and Jon Huntsman repudiated earlier endorsements of cap and trade legislation and sought to distance themselves from remedies for global warming. As governor of Utah Huntsman was a leading advocate of cap and trade to control greenhouse gases; now he thinks it would be damaging to the economy. As governor of Minnesota, Pawlenty also supported cap and trade; in a bow to the Republican Right, he appeared on Fox News to confess that he was wrong because it would harm the economy.

Most of the early candidates for the Republican nomination, however, seemed reluctant to make known their position on a proposed return of the country to the gold standard. In June 2011 Bachmann, former senator Rick Santorum of Pennsylvania, former House speaker Newt Gingrich, businessman Herman Cain, and former New Mexico governor Gary Johnson joined a bus tour organized by the Iowa Tea Party and American Principles in Action to debate monetary policy and to train Tea Party members in political activism. Only Johnson came out strongly in favor of a return to a monetary policy fixing the value of currency to the weight of gold, a system abandoned during the Nixon presidency. Bachmann said she would think about it. Interestingly, Congressman Ron Paul, the most ardent advocate of a return to the gold standard, did not take part.[6]

Tea Party influence has also registered strongly in states whose legislatures as a result of the 2010 elections contain heavy Republican majorities—none perhaps more so than Texas. Governor Rick Perry and the state legislature's Tea Party caucus enthusiastically pushed the party's agenda. The movement also exerted influence in the legislature through a citizens' Tea Party advisory committee working jointly with the governor and caucus.

To the delight of the Tea Party the Texas House passed a radical bill cutting $23 billion in state spending to balance the budget, raised no taxes, and gave in to Tea Party demands not to dip into the Rainy Day Fund. The legislature considered measures against illegal immigration and passed resolutions asserting state sovereignty and calling for an amendment to the federal constitution to require a balanced budget. Above all they fast-tracked an "emergency issue" requiring voter picture identification, a measure critics saw as an attempt not to prevent voter fraud but to suppress Democratic voting. Spending on public schools, already poorly funded, was slashed, along with Medicaid and a variety of other social programs.[7]

The influence of the Tea Party and the Christian Right could be seen too in Governor Perry's solidifying his relationship with both as he contemplated becoming a presidential candidate. Before entering the Republican presidential primaries, Perry on May 23, 2011, proclaimed August 6 a "Day of Prayer and Fasting for Our Nation's Challenges." This event reinforced Perry's already strong relationship with the Southern fundamentalist right, attracted national media attention, drew criticism from liberals (probably welcome), and bolstered his standing among evangelical Tea Partiers.

The Roots of the Tea Party's Grassroots

In his 1988 book *Middle American Individualism,* sociologist Herbert Gans wrote, "The middle American search for personal freedom means liberation from unwelcome cultural, social, political, and economic constraints, but also from a lack of economic as well as emotional security. Middle Americans, like most other Americans, want to be able to avoid involuntary conformity, whether it's required by the family, neighbors, or the government."[8] Thus twenty years before the Tea Party emerged Gans described a key element of the animating spirit of the movement's grassroots.

The Tea Party has attracted mostly highly partisan Republicans but also many individuals from across the political spectrum. Among its scattered unaffiliated groups are people who were previously independents or not involved in politics. Why do they gravitate to the Tea Party, and why do they get angrier at government and President Obama than at the Wall Street bankers and corporate executives who bore far more responsibility for the economic collapse and walked away with millions in pay and bonuses? Why do ordinary persons facing the same economic insecurities (think corporate downsizing) and environmental hazards emanating from poorly regulated corporations (think BP oil spill) gravitate to a free market ideology propagated by powerful interests that profit from damage to Main Street?

The wellsprings of these impulses lie deep in American culture, in its mythology and illusions, which are ingrained in the mentality of many citizens of various political persuasions. Antigovernment attitudes can be traced back to the American Revolution. So too can a negative populism that for most decades after the founding consisted of fear of centralized power and local communities responding to external threats posed by state or national government activity. Several developments in the early twenty-first century have combined to create anxieties that have also helped to generate a right-wing populist movement: government growth since 9/11, a staggering economic downturn, and a nation whose cultural makeup is rapidly changing, symbolized most vividly by its first African American president.

Moreover, since the 1970s both events and a well-organized campaign by corporations and libertarian billionaires working with, since the 1990s, right-wing radio and Fox News have combined to nurture hostility to the state. This well-funded campaign has worked relentlessly to associate the rhetoric of freedom and liberty with antigovernment impulses. A patina of popular indifference obscures the power of giant corporations, while unceasing efforts to limit the ability of government and unions to counterbalance the power of finance, industry, and capital saturate networks of information. Progressives possess fewer resources to shape popular perceptions and have devoted far less effort to defend programs that show government at its best.

Antigovernment forces also have crusaded continuously to create an antitax climate, helping to ingrain an explicit link between government "waste, fraud, and abuse" with taxes themselves. Though difficult to imagine now, perhaps, American political culture in the mid-twentieth century was far more tax-accepting. During World War II the government not only raised individual and corporate taxes to very high levels but also waged a propaganda campaign for taxation built around the theme of shared sacrifice. Hollywood stars and other celebrities appeared in newspapers and magazines and on the radio to remind citizens of the sacrifices of American servicemen and -women overseas and helped to create a "taxpaying culture."[9] Since the 1970s and 1980s, however, the Republican Party and more recently the new right-wing media have implanted an antitax dogmatism at the very core of their reason for being.

The amount of Americans' personal income dependent on taxes has grown as federal programs such as Social Security, Medicare, veterans' benefits, and unemployment compensation have consumed increasing amounts of tax dollars in recent decades. In 2009, according to the Bureau of Economic Analysis, when salaries for local, state, and federal employees are added to the total, "more than a quarter of all personal income in the United States is paid for with tax dollars."[10]

Seldom does any voice in the media, or even from Democrats or liberals (not always the same group), point to the worth of taxes in paying for safety (police and national defense), schools, health care, fire departments, protection of the nation's natural beauty, preservation of the national heritage, and much more. Those who point to their necessity rarely rise above defending them as a necessary evil. The contemporary antitax climate is not hospitable to U.S. Supreme Court Justice Louis D. Brandeis's observation that taxes are the price we pay for civilization.

Ironically, even as the state has underwritten the welfare of increasing numbers of citizens, the public's unawareness of what one political scientist has called the "submerged state" has also played a role. Thus benefits to citizens administered through private agencies or the tax system are not "visible." For example, in February 2009 the new administration granted tax credits worth $288 billion to 95 percent of taxpayers, but a year later only 12 percent believed they were paying lower taxes. On the contrary, 64 percent thought the president had raised taxes. Citizens receiving this type of credit, student loans, or mortgage interest subsidies usually respond that they "have not used a government social program." Submerged benefits are often successful but inconspicuous, so these programs do little to create favorable attitudes toward the government. Citizens are more positive to the government after using "visible social programs."[11]

The submerged state, according to political scientist Suzanne Mettler, "obscures the role of government and exaggerates that of the market." "Until political leaders reveal government benefits for what they are by talking openly about them," she adds, "we cannot have an honest discussion about spending, taxes, or deficits."[12]

There is a further irony, in that the very corporate interests funding antitax ideology usually benefit the most from hidden state subsidies. For example, three of the five states hauling in the most cash in agricultural subsidies are "red states" where antigovernment fever waxes strong; seven of the top ten subsidized states normally go Republican in elections.

Besides the antigovernment strain, the liberal tradition in the United States emphasizes the pursuit of self-interest, inspires moderate to little reverence for the collective, and holds sacred individual rights of self-expression. In addition, American egalitarianism does not inhibit but rather incites a scramble for wealth and status, with the end result being not resentment but envy and legitimization of the rich.[13] Fusion of egalitarianism with deference to the rich provides part of the answer as to why many people direct their anger at government and not at the gamblers of Wall Street.

According to historian Mark Lilla the Tea Party has incorporated—as have many other Americans—"the Sixties principle of private autonomy" and "the Eighties principle of economic autonomy." "For half a century now," he writes, "Americans have been rebelling in the name of individual freedom." This "libertarian eruption," as he terms it, has brought forth a populism that wants to neutralize government power and appeals powerfully to the freedom of individual choice. "It gives voice to those who feel they are being bullied, but this voice has only one Garbo-like thing to say: I want to be left alone."[14] Not entirely alone, one might say, because libertarianism with benefits means, "I want to be left alone, *selectively*."

Most analysts of the Tea Party, friends and foes alike, have tended to concentrate on how its adherents stand out from other citizens (being whiter, wealthier, older, and more educated than other Americans). But it can be equally instructive to examine how rank-and-file Tea Partiers resemble other Americans of whatever demographic group or political persuasion. Millions of Americans share the sense that they are losing control of their lives and that vast impersonal forces, some global in character, exert too much influence on their ability to live as they wish. Political philosopher Michael J. Sandel has identified this concern as one of the major causes of discontent. Another is "the sense that, from family to neighborhood to nation, the moral fabric of our community is unraveling around us." Add to that citizens' perception, rife since the 1960s and 1970s, that their government has grown ever more distant and unworthy of trust.[15]

Sandel locates the problem in a broad public philosophy of liberalism, one shared by all citizens across the political spectrum, which has replaced what he terms "republican liberty." This prevailing liberalism is not that of the welfare state and more equality but that of the obsession with individual rights—a freedom to pursue individual ends without regard for citizen responsibility to participate in self-government or the common good. Our earlier tradition of republican liberty harkened back to John Winthrop and the "city upon a hill." That tradition "gave heavy weight to collective rights and individual responsibility—more so than is given by our modern calculus of individual rights and collective responsibilities." In his marvelous history of Paul Revere and his fellow patriots in revolutionary Boston, historian David H. Fischer remarked: "We remember the individual rights, and forget the collective responsibilities."[16]

Our republican traditions also implied that public/political issues possessed a moral grounding, and Sandel faults contemporary progressives for ignoring this dimension. Consequently, "fundamentalists rush in where liberals fear to tread. . . . Absent a political agenda that addresses the moral dimension of public questions, attention becomes riveted on the private vices of public officials."[17] One need only tune in to daily cable "news" programs or consult the front page of today's newspaper to see evidence for that observation.

But conservatives who rail against government fail to see that a stronger state grew to counter powerful, unregulated, and often irresponsible economic forces. Conservatives and reactionaries "wrongly assume that rolling back the power of the national government would liberate individuals to pursue their own ends instead of leaving them at the mercy of economic forces beyond their control."[18]

Though their analysis of the problem may differ, the sense of lacking control over one's destiny engulfs Tea Partiers and other Americans alike. Similarly, the dysfunction of the national government dismays both liberals and conservatives. The impact of money on policy is all too evident, as is the power of lobbyists and special interest groups whose policy goals take precedence over those of majorities of citizens. Many Americans now know that due to archaic rules a minority in the Senate (or even just one member, in the case of a judicial appointment) has the ability to prevent any legislation from moving forward.[19]

Disillusionment with government "for the people" is hardly limited to Tea Partiers. Interviews with voters of both parties repeatedly reveal the conviction that government, in the end, works to the benefit of the well-connected, the wealthy, and, in the wake of the 2008 economic collapse, the irresponsible. Citizens feel "estranged" from government. Democratic voters in particular do not trust Democratic politicians' promises to work for the people.[20]

Not so obvious to the public is the "revolving jobs door" by which congressional staffers or representatives themselves move from government to lucrative positions lobbying for business and corporations. Between 2000 and 2010, 243 people worked on the House banking committee staff. Of them, 126 left the committee. Fully half of that number registered as lobbyists, mostly in the financial industry. Most of those people with expertise eventually went to work for the very interests they were formerly charged with regulating. One of the new lobbyists, Michael Paese, served as a top staffer for liberal Democratic congressman Barney Frank and worked on writing the new legislation aimed at regulating Wall Street. Today he works for Goldman Sachs.[21]

Among the multiple sources of dysfunction one must count the impact of politically inspired—to be frank, biased—media. A large majority of Tea Party supporters—63 percent—have said they get most of their political information and news from Fox News. Rupert Murdoch and Roger Ailes created it precisely to frame news and information from a right-wing point of view. While Fox News is hardly alone in contributing to the hyper-partisan political climate that so many Americans lament, surveys have often shown that its viewers hold more misperceptions about important issues than any other comparable group. Many Fox News viewers, for example, kept believing in the presence of weapons of mass destruction in Iraq long after a majority had been convinced otherwise. The Fox News engrossment in the Tea Parties as well as the Republican Party sets it apart because of the degree to which it contributes to ideological polarization. Roger Ailes's network cannot claim uniqueness in blurring the line between "news" and entertainment or in failing to take the trouble to pursue deep-background, avowedly impartial news reporting or investigative journalism. "Sensationalism," comments media critic Eric Alterman, "not substance, is what drives ratings."[22]

It is nevertheless difficult to discount the influence of right-wing talk radio and the Fox Network's propaganda machine. These media constitute a new and powerful weapon benefiting both corporate America and the Republican Party. They materially help to create rage at government and progressive political policies.

That rage has also created a potential pitfall for the grass-roots Tea Parties. Electing representatives to Congress and state legislatures who insist on purity of principle without negotiation or compromise runs the risk of creating a "practicality backlash" among voters, especially independents. The center of the American electorate usually prefers some sort of flexibility and political realism from lawmakers. In the wake of the debt ceiling standoff and its economic reverberations, the Tea Party's disapproval rating rose to 40 percent, the highest ever. Ironically, the grassroots constituency displayed more willingness to compromise than congressional Republicans.[23]

The Tea Partiers, finally, are routinely referred to in the media as conservatives. But their blend of astroturf and grassroots populism is more accurately labeled right-wing or reactionary populism. Besides wholesale reaction against government, the movement also expresses a "heartland" ethos of ethnocentrism among older white Americans experiencing rapid change in the kinds of people who make up the nation.

"We the people" are changing, and the evidence suggests that Tea Partiers are in part reacting to increasing racial and ethnic diversity. From 2000 to 2010 the Hispanic population accounted for more than half the growth in the total population of the United States. It grew by 43 percent from 35.3 million to 50.5 million, or from 13 percent of the total to 16 percent. The Asian population, though smaller, experienced the fastest rate of growth, increasing from 10.2 to 14.7 million.

Although the white population grew numerically by just over 2 million to 196.8 million, its rate of growth was the slowest of any group (1%), and its proportion of the total population decreased from 69 to 64 percent. Despite the slowdown in Hispanic immigration at the end of the decade because of economic decline, the nation's ever more noticeable diversity is proceeding apace.

The Census Bureau now pays increasing attention to persons in the "multiracial" category. Although numbering only 9 million (3% of the total), these individuals too portend a different America on the horizon—call it the Tiger Woods phenomenon.[24]

The Tea Party may not be reacting overtly to demographic change, and indeed many of its supporters protest that they are not. Yet hostile as well as neutral observers have commented often on its lack of diversity, especially with regard to African Americans. Certainly black conservatives exist within the Tea Party, but in July 2010 the National Association for the Advancement of Colored People, having perhaps seen too many signs at Tea Party rallies depicting President Obama as an African witch doctor, adopted a resolution condemning "racist elements" infiltrating the movement and called on its leaders to repudiate the fringe elements.

Tea Party leaders rejected the accusation, and conservative bloggers and some movement groups shot back that the NAACP itself was "racist." But then Tea Party groups began to emphasize their commitment to diversity, as did the newly formed Tea Party Congressional Caucus. On July 31 a movement coalition calling itself "Uni-Tea" held a Diversity Day in Philadelphia, featuring several prominent African American conservatives among the speakers. In September Freedom-Works launched a "Diverse Tea" website to promote diversity and to counter what it called liberals' "false allegations of racism."

By October these efforts by Tea Parties to eliminate racially offensive elements led NAACP President Benjamin Jealous to say that "the majority of Tea Party supporters are sincere, principled people of good will." Jealous also acknowledged the efforts of Tea Party leaders to promote diversity and welcomed the steps taken to weed out offensive images and actions at Tea Party rallies. But the comments came in his introduction to a NAACP report that called attention to some local Tea Party organizations being infiltrated by extremists. The report provided profiles of bigots active for years before the emergence of the Tea Party who had jumped on its bandwagon to promote their far-out ideologies. Jealous cautioned that these purveyors of prejudice did not characterize the great majority of decent people in the Tea Party.[25]

Any widespread populist movement attracts its share of fringe elements, and in this regard the Tea Parties resemble other decentralized protest movements. More troubling, however, are opinion surveys plumbing the attitudes of the rank and file toward racial and ethnic minorities and immigrants. While the majority of Tea Partiers are not vehemently hostile to President Obama's policies because of his race, racial resentment seems to influence the views of the minority of "birthers" in the movement who deny the president's legitimacy.

Tea Partiers are less favorably disposed to African Americans and Hispanics than most Americans, according to a 2010 University of Washington survey of whites in five states who approved of the Tea Party. Similarly the CBS News / *Times* poll found that 52 percent of Tea Partiers believe that too much has been made of problems facing black people, compared to 28 percent among all adults.[26]

A follow-up University of Washington survey of twelve states yielded similar results. The researchers regarded as most striking a divide between "mainstream" conservative Republicans and Tea Party Republicans. Significant differences also appeared between the two groups on the question of whether the president is a practicing Christian: 27 percent of Tea Partiers believed that the president is a practicing Muslim, compared to 16 percent of other conservatives, and 26 percent of Tea Partiers did not believe that the president had a valid birth certificate.[27]

That polling took place before April 2011, when the White House, seeking to quiet a new flurry of attention to the birth issue raised by potential candidates for the Republican presidential nomination, released the president's long-form birth certificate from Hawaii. Fox News, Rush Limbaugh, and others who had stirred the birther pot quickly backed off. In the space of about two weeks, the percentage of Republicans who believed the president was definitely or probably born in another country dropped from 24 percent to 13 percent.

For a recalcitrant minority, however, no document suffices. Their quarrel is not with the absence of a certificate but with the presence of the man himself. Savvy Tea Partiers recognize this as well as the likelihood that birther agitation can damage their image.

Similarly, hard-line nativist responses to immigrants by Tea Parties and other right-wing Republicans risk alienating a fast-growing and ever larger ethnic group—Latinos. Extreme anti-immigrant activists also have tried to exploit the Tea Party movement, and toleration of their presence in Tea Party ranks can only be regarded as an electoral gift to Democrats. At the same time many Americans who are not Tea Party supporters are frustrated with the failure of federal lawmakers during several administrations to create a policy to deal with illegal immigration and the presence of millions of undocumented immigrants in the country.

Nevertheless, Latinos now constitute one in six Americans, and increasing numbers of them are voting. In 2008 Latinos shifted massively away from Republicans. The group's turnout at the polls rose by a quarter, and 67 percent of them voted for Obama.[28]

The future of the Tea Parties may well lie in their responses to the nation's changing demographics. When the Census Bureau released its final 2010 results, one observer commented that it was "a postcard from the future." The nation's transformation into a "majority-minority" nation was proceeding faster than expected, especially among young people.[29]

The percentage of minority young people under 18 rose

from 39.1 percent of that cohort ten years earlier to 46.5 percent in 2010. Demographers had already predicted that minorities would make up a majority of the under-18 population by 2020. Because this young population will soon form families and have children, the nonwhite part of the whole likely will grow even faster. The nonwhite tilt of the youth population has profound political implications for the future. "The young, increasingly minority population is likely to view public investment in schools, health care, and infrastructure as critical to its economic prospects, while the predominantly white senior population might be increasingly reluctant to fund such services through taxes."

Besides the young and minorities, unmarried women also are likely to support government intervention in the economy. That group too is growing and along with Latinos and African Americans made up 43 percent of the total electorate in 2008 and voted 62 percent for Obama.

Meanwhile the antitax Tea Parties strongly express reluctance to fund investment in health, education, and welfare, much less in the "social safety net" for the disadvantaged. At some point in the not-too-distant future, however, the nation's electorate will begin increasingly to reflect the changing character of the population as well as the concerns of a younger electorate. Those voters likely will be flexible and tolerant on social issues and more open to government activism, and eventually they will outnumber the votes coming from Tea Party supporters.[30]

Aside from the challenges posed to the Tea Parties by a changing population and electorate, there also exists the potential for conflict between the evangelical right with its insistence on promoting cultural issues and the libertarian/free market wing (and its corporate backers) focused on economic issues to the exclusion of divisive moral questions. In addition the movement may encounter a weakening of the grassroots base because of problems that have arisen often in the life cycle of populist movements.

Historically, populist movements that have entered the political arena have usually experienced a growing rift between leaders and followers: the former become more professionalized while the grassroots true believers react to that distancing with disillusion and withdrawal. Thus far only faint signs of this tension have become visible.

But the Tea Parties also have generated an additional source of separation between the leadership and the rank and file: they have become highly successful money-making machines. Marketing companies having little or nothing to do with the political efforts of the movement have been selling products with a "Tea Party" brand: buttons, flags, watches, thongs, skateboards, bobbleheads, bumper stickers, jewelry, golf club towels, T-shirts, and more. The head of marketing at Zazzle .com, an online customized products maker, commented that his company by November 2010 had sold "thousands of Tea Party items worth millions of dollars." Some marketers advertise their products on websites that purport to be activist parts of the movement. These free riders, as well as companies like Zazzle, have encountered legal action from the Tea Party Patriots who claim control over the domain names being used. The Patriots found it necessary to warn their membership against "Tea Party" websites that have been "collecting data and donations" from supporters "across the nation . . . to market more and collect more data which they make available to advertisers through News.Max."[31]

From within the ranks of the Patriots themselves, in addition, disgruntled former activists wonder if the national leaders, Mark Meckler and Jenny Beth Martin, have succumbed to the seductions of Beltway culture and have been tempted to exploit the movement themselves. The Patriots have hired three high-powered fundraising firms with strong ties to the Republican Party as well as Christian Right groups. One of them, MDS Communications, based in Arizona, works for the Republican National Committee; it is reported to keep at least 70 percent of the money it raises. When the Tea Party Patriots received an anonymous gift of one million dollars, Meckler announced that it would be distributed to local chapters but then asked the locals to turn over their membership lists to the national organization, which were then put to use by the fundraising firms. The national coordinators further have refused to open their account books to the membership; while the group claims to be a tax-exempt charity, donations from members have not been deductible for a period of at least two years as the Patriots did not apply during that time to the IRS for such status. The leaders' secretiveness regarding finances seems anomalous in a group demanding financial accountability from government.[32]

The former activists who have raised questions about the organization's finances say they do not know the salaries of the national coordinators or staff members. They are troubled also by the role of Jenny Beth Martin's husband Lee as the national official in charge of managing the group's money—his title is assistant treasurer. Aside from raising concern among the Martins' critics about a conflict of interest, Lee Martin's business history increases their doubts. Up until 2007 he had owned for several years a Georgia company that recruited immigrant workers from Central and South America and supplied them to Atlanta-area businesses. These minimum wage temporary workers usually spoke no English and worked mostly in food processing. The company went bankrupt, and meanwhile Martin had failed to pay hundreds of thousands of dollars in payroll taxes and owed the IRS $510,000 and the state of Georgia $172,000.[33]

The Martins have rebounded very well from earlier setbacks. Jenny Beth now has her own website separate from that of the Patriots, and in 2010 *Time* named her one of the one hundred most influential persons in the world. Before the 2010 midterm elections she and Meckler traveled around the country in a corporate jet provided by a wealthy Republican benefactor, behavior that also provoked complaints from the grassroots.

Both the Martins and Meckler had been active in Republican Party politics before the Tea Party came along. Meckler, who appears regularly on Fox News and is routinely sought after by reporters for sound bites, also had been involved in a controversial company, Herbalife, that critics say operates much like a pyramid scheme. But what matters now is the possibility that grassroots Tea Party Patriot supporters will come to perceive its leadership as becoming indistinguishable from the Republican Party establishment, not to mention seeing it as the profit-making enterprise decried by liberal bloggers and former activists.

In the nineteenth century grassroots populist movements that turned to politics often became undermined by political party establishments offering patronage in the form of jobs or political advancement. In recent decades the range of inducements available to coopt populist leaders have expanded and include not just celebrity but also the immensely potent possibility of personal monetary gain.

The grassroots Tea Parties may remain independently active, or they may fade into the Republican Party, not quietly, in any case influencing the party's agenda for years to come. The corporate astroturf "Tea Parties," of course, along with their Congressional and lobbyist enablers, have been with us for decades and will remain behind the curtain to work their wizardry of libertarianism with benefits.

THE FIRST
TEA PARTY

IN A NICE IRONY OF HISTORY the Boston Tea Party of 1773—about which so much is said and so little known—resulted in part from an attempted bailout of a large international company on the verge of bankruptcy—the East India Company. The British government, already heavily involved in the company's management and finances, assumed virtual control and then coupled a plan to rescue it with a scheme to raise revenue from the American colonies. The bailout, however, was incidental to the main question that had put Britain and her colonies on a collision course since 1765: the British Parliament's claim of sovereignty over the colonies and its right to regulate and tax American commerce.

After Britain's victory in the French and Indian War, which gave it mastery over the North American continent, a succession of ministers and Parliament together set out to reorganize the imperial system and to require the colonies to help pay for their defense. Britain's initial try at raising revenue from the colonies, the Stamp Act of 1765, brought forth a wave of violent mob and crowd protests throughout the colonies, the organization of the Sons of Liberty, and an agreement among the colonies to stop importing British goods. Parliament backed down but asserted its right to legislate for the colonies "in all cases whatsoever." The episode also generated the cry of "no taxation without representation" and, more important, a growing perception that Britain did not extend to the colonies the rights and respect properly due British subjects.

In 1767 Parliament again tried to raise revenue from the colonies by passing the Townshend Act, which placed duties on glass, paper, lead, painters' colors, and tea. It also tightened measures against smuggling, common throughout its Atlantic provinces, and declared the purpose of the act to raise revenue to pay the salaries of colonial officials, thus making them independent of colonial legislatures.[1]

Opposition, though in a lower key to that of 1765, spread throughout the colonies generating petitions of protest, especially from merchants; boycotts of British goods; and a partially successful anti-tea campaign, particularly strong in New England. New York, Philadelphia, and points south managed to boycott tea from England more easily because most of the tea they were consuming had been smuggled from Holland. Boston depended primarily on tea from Britain, so while the volume of tea imported into New England fell, the boycott there was only partially and sporadically successful. During the years after 1768 this situation caused tea in New England to become "a marked commodity," a constant reminder of Parliament's claim to tax the colonies "at its pleasure."[2]

The boycotts nevertheless generated enough economic pressure from merchants in London to cause Parliament to repeal all of the Townshend Act (1770) *except* for the duty on tea as a symbol of parliamentary authority. This broke down colonial unity, and imports from Britain increased to levels above those before non-importation. Bostonians increased their imports of tea under continued but milder protest. But the years from 1770 to 1773 marked a period of relative calm in British-colonial relations.

Enter the East India Company, whose looming financial

crisis and close ties with and regulation by the British government "inadvertently precipitated the final crisis between Parliament and the American colonies." To relieve the company of its enormous debt and to dispose of its huge surplus of tea—as well as to raise revenue from the colonies—Parliament's Tea Act of 1773 provided that the British government would refund to the company the export duty of 12 pence per pound and instead would charge a 3 pence duty on tea shipped to the colonies, payable at colonial ports. The Chancellor of the Exchequer, Lord North, calculated that the colonists would pay the tax since they would be able to buy tea more cheaply than English consumers. North calculated wrongly and, worse, arranged for designated agents to replace the colonial merchants who previously had served as middlemen.[3]

In Massachusetts the stubborn royal governor Thomas Hutchinson fueled more resentment by appointing two of his sons as tea agents. Indeed, Hutchinson had disturbed the period of calm in Massachusetts by dealing with the local resistance—the Patriot party—in his typically high-handed way and asserting in January 1773 before the colony's general court Parliament's authority over American legislatures.

As reports of the Tea Act spread through the colonies in the months after its passage in May, a widespread resistance to the plan had emerged by October, resting on the convictions that if the tea tax was accepted other taxes would follow and that the East India Company's monopoly on tea would lead to its establishing monopolies on all other goods. The inter-colonial "Committees of Correspondence" (shadow governments organized by Patriots) and the Sons of Liberty sprang into action. Resistance at New York and Philadelphia forced the company agents to resign, and the ships turned around. At Charleston, South Carolina, the tea made its way into warehouses, only for some of it to be destroyed later and some to be sold by colonial rebels.

Boston followed a more radical path, one embraced by virtually the entire community except for the small number of loyalists in their midst. Governor Hutchinson, whose relations with the Patriot party had long since turned hostile (his house had been ransacked in the turmoil provoked by the Stamp Act), decided to rely on the military resources at his disposal to force a confrontation. The Patriots, gladly obliging him, put forth their demands soon after the first of three tea ships arrived, the *Dartmouth*.

On November 29 a huge assemblage at Faneuil Hall, not a town meeting but one open to all inhabitants, including many from surrounding towns, resolved that the ship must return to England. But the governor and the consignees remained adamant, and negotiations between the Patriots and the *Dartmouth*'s owner went nowhere.

Tensions grew as fear spread throughout the citizenry that Hutchinson would resort to force. Indeed, one observer remarked that one could not buy pistols in the town, as they "are all bought up, with a determination to repel force by force." Two more mass meetings followed in December as the day approached when the customs officers would be required to unload the tea.

The final citizens' meeting, on December 16, began at ten in the morning in a cold rain, with some five thousand souls crowded into Old South Church and spilling out the doorways, and continued throughout the day. At nearly six in the evening, as darkness fell, with no sign that the *Dartmouth* would set sail, Samuel Adams rose to say that he did not see what more could be done "to save our country." Immediately someone let out a war whoop, and cries went up: "Boston Harbor a teapot tonight," and "The Mohawks are come." Some men in the rear were already wearing light Indian disguises, with dabs of paint and old blankets; others had covered their faces with soot or burnt cork.[4]

Down to the waterfront went some thirty to fifty men including those in on the planning, others who were volunteers informed of the event, plus a few young men "swept up in the excitement." They rapidly split into three groups at Griffin's Wharf and boarded the three tea ships. Gradually a huge silent crowd gathered near the wharf to watch. By nine o'clock, in a little less than three hours, the "Mohawks" had dumped some £10,000 worth of tea into the harbor—a huge sum and, in the eyes of Parliament, a shocking destruction of property.[5]

The "Mohawks" did not undertake this daring venture for personal profit, as an incident on board one of the ships strikingly revealed. A young shoemaker who joined the party noticed a certain "Captain O'Connor" of his acquaintance board the ship and fill his pockets and coat lining with tea. The shoemaker informed the "Mohawk" in charge of his crew of this attempt at looting, and the men removed O'Connor roughly from the vessel, tearing his coat off in the process. The next day, the Patriots nailed it to a whipping post near his home to shame the would-be thief.[6]

Boston's patriot party originally did not intend to destroy the tea but turned to it "probably" as "a last resort." But they carried out the venture with superb planning and for decades afterward guarded carefully the identity of those who had participated in such a provocative action.[7]

Boston had already been the epicenter of colonial protest for several years, with the result that since 1768 two regiments of British redcoats had been quartered in Boston. Tension between the soldiers and townspeople had resulted in the "Boston Massacre" of 1770, and Parliament viewed Boston and Massachusetts as different from other colonies, a hornet's nest of defiance and rebellion.

Parliament retaliated with the Coercive Acts: closing the port of Boston until it paid for the tea; allowing the governor to transfer to England the trial of any official accused of an offense in the line of duty; a new Quartering Act opening up private homes as lodging for redcoats, if needed; and, in an assault on one of New England's most cherished institutions, eliminating local town government in the colony. Instead of isolating Boston, however, these harsh measures united the colonies to rally around Massachusetts.

Historians agree that the Boston Tea Party marked a pivotal event on the road to rebellion. From that point on, particularly after the passage of the Coercive Acts, "insurgency" spread throughout Massachusetts and other colonies. The party was a radical act: "a quasi-military action," bold and dangerous and "the most revolutionary act of the decade in Boston." The planners and the participants all risked arrest and prosecution.[8]

Indeed, Bostonians at the time did not sanitize the event as a "tea party" but referred to it as "the destruction of the tea." Historian Alfred H. Young has shown that the "tea party" rubric did not come into use until four decades later.

The action was populist and an act of virtually the entire community, approved by "the whole body of the people" of Boston, not just a minority of militants. John Adams, a lawyer of moderate temperament and regarded by many as a conservative, believed "the Destruction of the Tea" was necessary. For it to land would have accepted the principle of taxation by a distant Parliament "against which the Continent have struggled for 10 years." He wrote further in his diary, "There is a Dignity, a Majesty, a Sublimity, in this effort of the Patriots that I greatly admire. The People should never rise, without doing something to be remembered—something notable and striking. This destruction of the Tea is so bold, so daring, so firm, intrepid and inflexible, and it must have so important Consequences, and so lasting, that I can't but consider it as an Epocha in History."[9]

Almost two and half centuries later, to recognize that Tea Party politicians and supporters are dependent on government programs that provide security, benefits, and subsidies is to point to the many ways that the economy and the American quality of life depend on the federal government. Tea Party supporters may be no more or less hypocritical than other Americans, though it is difficult to resist applying that word to certain politicians. Tea Party supporters are no less intelligent than other Americans, and some of them are better informed. Inconsistent policy positions are not limited to the Tea Parties' grassroots but also extend to an electorate that is ideologically conservative and programmatically liberal.

Libertarianism with benefits can be described as having your cake and eating it too. At the grassroots it springs from lack of awareness of government programs pumping money into the economy as well as unwillingness to recognize the many ways in which the government improves everyone's lives. But it fosters a politics that obscures identifying the real winners and losers of policy outcomes. Politicians who denounce big government as "socialism" but rake in corporate welfare do their constituents no favor by hiding or obfuscating their personal involvement in "big government" and "spending."

★　★　★

The Boston Tea Party launched Americans into the future, some knowing but others perhaps only dimly realizing that from then on there might be no turning back. In 1773 independence was not yet on the minds of the Patriots, and they slowly, often reluctantly, came to the point of a complete rupture with Britain. Bostonians and their fellow colonials engaged in resistance to the empire, although in the process of becoming insurgents, were insisting on their rights as British subjects, as freeborn Englishmen.

In doing so, they looked not backward but forward, to an uncertain future. Theirs was a populism of the ordered community, in which liberty meant individual freedom to pursue one's destiny as well as responsibility and a regard for the common good.

Notes

Chapter 1. Reading Tea Leaves

   1. After deciding on the title for this chapter, I discovered Francis S. Drake's *Tea Leaves: Being a Collection of Letters and Documents Relating to the Shipment of Tea to the American Colonies in the year 1773, by the East India Tea Company* (Boston: A. O. Crane, 1884). Books favorable to the Tea Party include Dick Armey and Matt Kibbe, *Give Us Liberty: A Tea Party Manifesto* (New York: William Morrow, 2010) and Scott Rasmussen and Doug Schoen, *Mad as Hell: How the Tea Party Movement Is Fundamentally Remaking Our Two-Party System* (New York: Harper, 2010). For a critical view of the movement's "anti-history," see Jill Lepore, *The Whites of Their Eyes: The Tea Party's Revolution and the Battle over American History* (Princeton: Princeton University Press, 2010).

   2. Devon Burghart and Leonard Zeskind, "Tea Party Nationalism," Institute for Research and Education on Human Rights, Special Report, Fall 2010, available at www.teapartynationalism.com/pdf/TeaParty Nationalism.pdf (hereafter, Burghart and Zeskind, IREHR Report). Polls have varied during 2009–2011 regarding support for the Tea Party. Stephanie Condon, "Poll: Tea Party Activists Small But Passionate Group," CBS News, April 14, 2010, available at www.cbsnews.com/8301 -503544_162-20002536-503544.html.

   3. Chris LeSeur, "Letter to the editor," *Lexington Herald-Leader,* May 17, 2011; Marc Lacey, "In Arizona, Tea Party License Plate Draws Opposition from Its Honorees," *New York Times,* May 4, 2011.

   4. Matt Bai, "D.I.Y. Populism, Left and Right," *New York Times,* October 30, 2010.

   5. Kate Zernike, *Boiling Mad: Inside Tea Party America* (New York: Times Books, 2010), 119. Zernike's balanced account concentrates on individual activists.

   6. Mark Blumenthal, "Tea Party: Polls Show Importance to GOP Base," *Huffington Post,* July 15, 2011, available at www.huffingtonpost .com/2011/07/15/tea-party-polls-show-impo_n_899901.html.

   7. Jack Kerwick, "The Tea Partier vs. The Republican," *The Moral Liberal,* May 24, 2011, available at www.themoralliberal.com/2011/05 /24/the-tea-partier-vs-the-republican/. See, e.g., Richard A. Viguerie,

Conservatives Betrayed: How George W. Bush and Other Big Government Conservatives Hijacked the Conservative Cause (Los Angeles: Bonus Books, 2006).

8. Available at www.gallup.com/poll/141119/debt-gov-power-among -tea-party-supporters-top-concerns.aspx.

9. "Leviathan Stirs Again," *The Economist,* January 21, 2010.

10. Paul C. Light, "Fact Sheet on the New True Size of Government," Brookings Institution, 2003.

11. Available at www.pollingreport.com/institut.htm#Federal.

12. "Public Wants Changes in Entitlements, Not Benefits," Pew Research Center, July 7, 2011, available at http://people-press.org/2011/07 /07/public-wants-changes-in-entitlements-not-change-in-benefits/.

13. Ronald P. Formisano, *For the People: American Populist Movements from the Revolution to the 1850s* (Chapel Hill: University of North Carolina Press, 2008).

14. Christopher Lasch, *The True and Only Heaven: Progress and Its Critics* (New York: W.W. Norton, 1991), 172–80.

15. 1892 Populist Party Platform (July 4, 1892).

16. Report quoted in Chrystia Freeland, "The Tea Party vs. 'The Freeloaders,'" *New York Times,* July 7, 2011. A forthcoming book was not available at the time of this writing.

17. Robin Abcarian, "Jobless Workers Dispute Claim from Tea Party and the Right that Benefits Foster Complacency," *Los Angeles Times,* September 23, 2010; Catherine Rampell, "Somehow, the Unemployed Became Invisible," *New York Times,* July 9, 2011.

18. Margaret Canovan, "Taking Politics to the People: Populism as the Ideology of Democracy," in *Democracies and the Populist Challenge,* ed. Yves Mény and Yves Surel (New York: Palgrave, 2002), 3.

19. Alan Ware, "The United States: Populism as a Political Strategy," in *Democracies and the Populist Challenge,* ed. Mény and Surel, 119.

Chapter 2. The Rise of the Tea Party

1. Kate Zernike, "Unlikely Activist Who Got to the Tea Party Early," *New York Times,* February 27, 2009.

2. See Dick Armey and Matt Kibbe, *Give Us Liberty: A Tea Party Manifesto* (New York: William Morrow, 2010). In the early 1970s liberal anti–Vietnam War activists called for tea party protests against military spending and corporate welfare. Jeremy Rifkin and John Rossen, *How to Commit Revolution American Style* (Secaucus, NJ: Lyle Stuart, 1973).

3. Burghart and Zeskind, IREHR Report, 15. In 1973 the Libertarian Party suggested sending tea bags to Congress. In 1980 it broached the idea of an antitax tea party. Between 1986 and 1993 this was a repeated notion of Citizens for a Sound Economy.

4. The promotions profited Fox, making 2009 its best year, with ratings rising 20 percent over 2008.

5. On Beck, see Sean Wilentz, "Confounding Fathers: The Tea Party's Cold War Roots," *The New Yorker,* October 18, 2010.

6. Beth Reinhard, "Iowa's Tea Party Kingmaker," *The Atlantic Monthly,* available at www.theatlantic.com/politics/archive/2011/03 /iowas-tea-party-kingmaker/72435/.

7. Matea Gold, "Sal Russo, the Firepower behind the 'Tea Party,'" *Los Angeles Times,* September 18, 2010.

8. Burghart and Zeskind, IREHR Report, 54; Kenneth P. Vogel, "GOP Operatives Crash the Tea Party," *Politico,* April 14, 2010, available at www.politico.com/news/stories/0410/35785.html. Some local Patriots chapters are also militia groups, and others have been exploited by extremist elements such as white nationalists who are "on the periphery" in some locales. Burghart and Zeskind, IREHR Report, 46–47.

Chapter 3. Political Payoff in the 2010 Midterm Elections

1. Sam Stein, "Scott Brown Finds Himself on Tea Party's 2012 Hit List," *Huffington Post,* November 3, 2010, available at www.huffing tonpost.com/2010/11/03/scott-brown-finds-himself_n_778269.html; Jennifer Epstein, "Tea Party Leader Lashes Out at Scott Brown," *Politico,* April 1, 2011, available at www.politico.com/news/stories/0411/52391 .html.

2. Available at www.politifact.com/search/?q=President+Obama +says+foreign+money.

3. Robert Draper, "How Kevin McCarthy Wrangles the Tea Party in Washington," *New York Times Magazine,* July 13, 2011.

4. Sheryl Gay Stolberg, "Roots of Bachmann's Ambition Began at Home," *New York Times,* June 21, 2011; Stolberg, "For Bachmann, Gay Rights Stand Reflects Mix of Issues and Faith," *New York Times,* July 16, 2011.

5. Quoted in Jennifer Steinhauer, "Conservative Congressman's Star Power Extends beyond District," *New York Times,* April 28, 2011.

6. Kevin Phillips, *American Theocracy: The Perils and Politics of Radical Religion, Oil, and Borrowed Money in the 21st Century* (New York: Viking, 2006), 102.

7. Although 2004 became known as the "moral values" election because 22 percent of voters said that the issue had influenced their vote, subsequent analysis showed that the ballot initiatives mobilized voters on both sides and may have broken to Kerry's benefit. Stephen Ansolabehere and Charles Stewart III, "Truth In Numbers," *Boston Review,* February/March 2005, available at www.bostonreview.net/BR30.1 /ansolastewart.php.

8. Samuel G. Freedman, "Evangelical, and Young, and Active in New Area," *New York Times,* November 28, 2009.

9. Laurie Goodstein, "Obama Made Gains among Younger Evangelical Voters, Data Shows," *New York Times,* November 7, 2008.

Chapter 4. The Tea Party and the Religious Right

1. *New York Times* / CBS Poll; Kate Zernike and Megan Thee-Brenan, "Poll Finds Tea Party Backers Wealthier and More Educated," *New York Times,* April 14, 2010.

2. Burghart and Zeskind, IREHR Report, 78.

3. Sarah Posner, "Tea Party Values," *The Nation,* September 21, 2010. On Southern Baptists, see Paul Harvey, *Freedom's Coming: Religious Culture and the Shaping of the South from the Civil War through the Civil Rights Era* (Chapel Hill: University of North Carolina Press, 2005).

4. Jerry Reth, "Christine O'Donnell 2010 Values Voters Summit in Washington," September 17, 2010, available at www.newsopi.com /politics/christine-odonnell-2010-values-voters-summit-in-washington -d-c-speech/4323/.

5. David Frum, "Christine O'Donnell's Misconceptions of the Constitution," *Washington Post,* October 22, 2010.

6. Justin Elliott, "Tea Partyers Gone Wild!" February 21, 2011, available at www.salon.com/news/politics/war_room/2011/02/21 /state_laws.

7. "Poll Examines Tea Party Faith Values," *Oregon Faith Report,* October 11, 2010, available at http://oregonfaithreport.com/2010/10 /poll-examines-tea-party-faith-values/print/.

8. Scott Clement and John C. Green, "The Tea Party, Religion and Social Issues," February 23, 2011, Pew Forum on Religion and Social Issues, available at http://pewresearch.org/pubs/1903/tea-party -movement-religion-social-issues-conservative-christian.

9. John M. Broder, "Obama Courting Evangelicals Once Loyal to Bush," *New York Times,* July 1, 2008; Ted Roelofs, "Will Evangelicals Reward Barack Obama for Reaching Out to Them," *Grand Rapids Press,* July 18, 2008.

10. Quotation from Amy Sullivan, "Are Evangelicals Really Sold on Palin?" *Time,* September 6, 2008; "Younger Evangelicals Split over Palin Pick," Associated Press, September 14, 2008, available at www.msnbc .msn.com/id/26704362/.

11. Jonathan Chait, "Rick Perry, Michelle Bachmann, and the Christian Right," *The New Republic,* July 5, 2011.

12. "LePage to NAACP: 'Kiss My Butt,' " *Portland Press Herald / Maine Sunday Telegram,* January 15, 2011; C. J. Ciaramella, "From the Streets to the Governor's Mansion, Paul LePage Embraces Fiscal Conservatism

for Survival," *The Daily Caller,* July 25, 2011; Sasha Abramsky, "Turning LePage," *The Nation,* July 18/25, 2011.

13. Kathleen Hennessey, " 'Tea Party' Rhetoric Steals the Stage at GOP Conference," *Los Angeles Times,* February 19, 2010.

Chapter 5. The Tea Party and Big Business

1. "Democracy Index 2010, Democracy in Retreat," Economist Intelligence Unit, available at http://graphics.eiu.com/PDF/Democracy _Index_2010_wed.pdf.

2. Public Religion Research Institute, "Plurality of Americans Believe Capitalism at Odds with Christian Values," April 2011. For the full results of the survey, see http://publicreligion.org/research/2011 /04/plurality-of-americans-believe-capitalism-at-odds-with-christian -values.

3. Lee Fang, "Asked If Untaxed Corporations Like Exxon Are Taxed Too Much, Tea Party Leaders Say Yes," *Think Progress,* November 3, 2010, available at http://thinkprogress.org/politics/2010/11/03/128196 /tea-party-corporations/.

4. Allison Kilkenny, "2/3rds of U.S. Corporations Pay Zero Federal Taxes: U.S. Uncut Movement Builds to Make Them Pay Up," *The Nation,* March 27, 2011, available at www.alternet.org/story/150387/2_3rds_of _us_corporations_pay_zero_federal_taxes%3A_us_uncut_movement _builds_to_make_them_pay_up.

5. The preceding paragraphs are based on Mike McIntire, "Odd Alliance: Business Lobby and Tea Party," *New York Times,* March 30, 2011.

6. Kate Zernike, "Tea Party Disputes Take Toll on Convention," *New York Times,* January 26, 2010; "Tea Party Nation," available at www .sourcewatch.org/index.php?title=Tea_Party_Nation.

7. Lisa Lerer and John McCormick, "Why Business Doesn't Trust the Tea Party," *Bloomberg Businessweek,* October 13, 2010, available at www.businessweek.com/print/magazine/content/10_43/b420006617 0117.htm.

8. Quotation from Gail Russell Chaddock, "Tea Party Faces Unusual Opponent in National Debt Limit Battle," *Christian Science Monitor,* May 16, 2011, available at www.csmonitor.com/USA/Politics/2011/0516 /Tea-party-faces-unusual-opponent-in-national-debt-limit-battle; Robert Reich, "Debt Limit at Heart of GOP's Impending Civil War," *San Francisco Gate,* May 27, 2011, available at http://articles.sfgate.com/2011 -05-29/opinion/29593401_1_debt-limit-national-debt-tea-partiers.

9. Quotation from "The New Republican Landscape," *New York Times,* April 18, 2011.

10. "Public Wants a Debt Ceiling Compromise, Expects a Deal before Deadline," Pew Research Center, July 26, 2011, available at http://people

-press.org/2011/07/26/public-wants-a-debt-ceiling-compromise-expects
-a-deal-before-deadline/; Kate Zernike, "That Monolithic Tea Party Just
Wasn't There," *New York Times,* August 1, 2011.

11. Jackie Calmes, "Pressuring Obama, House Bars Rise for Debt Ceiling," *New York Times,* May 31, 2011; Dana Milbank, "Muskets in Hand,
Tea Party Blasts House Republicans," *Washington Post,* May 9, 2011.

12. Raymond Hernandez, "Hoping Third Party Is Charm, Industrialist
Jolts House Race," *New York Times,* May 16, 2011; Raymond Hernandez,
"Democrat Wins Western New York Congressional Race," May 24, 2011,
available at http://thecaucus.blogs.nytimes.com/2011/05/24/heavy
-turnout-in-new-york-congressional-election/; "NY-26: Why Democrat
Kathy Hochul's Win Is Not Easily Minimized," *Daily Kos,* May 29, 2011,
available at www.dailykos.com/story/2011/05/29/980405/-NY-26:-Why
-Democrat-Kathy-Hochuls-win-is-not-easily-minimized.

13. Jennifer Steinhauer, "Democrats Take Aim at G.O.P. Freshmen on
Medicare," *New York Times,* May 16, 2011, available at http://thecaucus
.blogs.nytimes.com/2011/05/16/democrats-target-g-o-p-freshmen
-on-medicare; Tom Curry, "For GOP First Termer, a Mixed Reaction
on Medicare Vote," May 17, 2011, available at www.msnbc.msn.com/id
/43060806/ns/politics-capitol_hill/; Lucia Graves, "House Republicans
Face Backlash at Home over Medicare Vote," May 17, 2011, *Huffington
Post,* available at www.huffingtonpost.com/2011/05/17/house-republicans
-face-backlash-medicare_n_863144.html.

14. Quotation from Kate Zernike, "Tea Party Finds Power Leads to
Policy Splits," *New York Times,* June 28, 2011.

15. Jim Geraghty, "A Short History of the Tea Parties," January 28,
2011, available at www.nationalreview.com/blogs/print/258258.

Chapter 6. Frustration with Politics as Usual

1. Michael Kazin, *The Populist Persuasion: An American History*
(Ithaca: Cornell University Press, 1998; revised edition), 273.

2. Jeffrey A. Karp, "Explaining Public Support for Legislative Term
Limits," *Public Opinion Quarterly* 59 (Autumn 1995): 386.

3. Caroline J. Tolbert, John A. Grummel, and Daniel A. Smith, "The
Effect of Ballot Initiatives on Voter Turnout in the American States,"
American Politics Research 29 (November 2001): 625–48; Stephanie
Limb, "Special Interests Hiding behind 'Grassroot' Ballot Items," *Albion
Monitor,* available at www.albionmonitor.com/9703a/initiatives.html.

4. Paul West, "Rep.-Elect Harris Snagged in Health Care Flap," *Baltimore Sun,* November 16, 2010. In Congress Harris has been adamant
about repealing the health law and privatizing Medicare.

5. James Warren, "A Tea Party Congressman Cultivates His Base,"
New York Times, April 15, 2011.

6. Dana Milbank, "Forget Tea Party Rhetoric—Pork Barrel Politics Is Back," *Washington Post,* December 15, 2010.

7. At a town meeting in early June Duffy too was confronted by protesters and outbursts over his vote to change Medicare, and already in April Democrat Patrick "Pat" Kreitlow, a former state senator and television news anchor, announced that he would challenge Duffy in 2012. Rachel Rose Hartman, "Dems Excoriate Rep. Sean Duffy for 'Struggle' on Congressional Salary," *The Ticket,* March 30, 2011, available at http://news.yahoo.com/blogs/ticket/dems-excoriate-rep-sean-duffy-struggle-congressional-salary-20110330-092116-477.html.

8. Milbank, "Forget Tea Party Rhetoric."

9. "Kristi Noem," Wikipedia entry, available at http://en.wikipedia.org/wiki/Kristi_Noem; "Ag Subsidies with a Twist of Noem," *Constant Conservative,* August 9, 2010, available at www.constantconservative.com/2010/ag-subsidies-with-a-twist-of-Noem.

10. "Stephen Fincher," Wikipedia entry, available at http://en.wikipedia.org/wiki/Stephen_Fincher; Alex Pareene, "Shocker: Tea Party Congress Members Take Tons of Farm Subsidies," *Salon,* March 31, 2011, available at http://mobile.salon.com/politics/war_room/2011/03/31/welfare_tea_parties/index.html.

11. Bill Thompson, "Stearns Joins Bachmann's Tea Party Caucus on Capitol Hill," available at www.ocala.com/article/20100722/article/7221011?p=48tc=pg; Donna Marsh, "American Shame," *Huff Post New York,* April 23, 2011, available at www.huffingtonpost.com/donna-marsh-o/911-first-responders_b_852719.html; Eric Lipton, "Republicans Sought Clean Energy Money for Home States," *New York Times,* September 19, 2011.

12. Nick Wing, "Tea Party Billionaire David Koch Throwing Party for Congressional Republicans," *Huff Post Politics,* January 6, 2011, available at www.huffingtonpost.com/2011/01/05/david-koch-tea-party-republicans_n_804997.html; John Aloysius Farrell, "Koch Industries' Web of Influence," *Huff Post Business,* April 6, 2011, available at www.huffingtonpost.com/2011/04/06/koch-industries-web-of-influence_n_845306.html; Igor Volsky, "Koch Industries Applies for Federal Funds from Health Care Law It Opposes," August 31, 2010, available at http://thinkprogress.org/health/2010/08/31/171628/koch-earlyretiree/.

13. The EWG or Environmental Working Group Farm Subsidy Database is a treasure trove of information regarding subsidies including breakdowns by state and congressional districts. See http://farm.ewg.org/.

14. Thomas Byrne Edsall, "The Obama Coalition," *The Atlantic Monthly,* April 2010.

15. Marie Diamond, "After Promising to End Earmarks, Tea Party Freshmen Hog Defense Pork," *Think Progress,* May 26, 2011, available at http://thinkprogress.org/2011/05/26/defense-pork-tea-party/.

16. Lerer and McCormick, "Why Business Doesn't Trust the Tea Party," 6.

17. Zernike, *Boiling Mad,* 9. Zernike added that the sixty-two-year-old California woman had heart trouble and would eventually need Medicare. "'I guess I misspoke,' she said. 'I didn't look at it from the perspective from losing things I need. I think I've changed my mind.'"

Chapter 7. The Tea Party and American Political Culture

1. Zachary Courser, "The Tea Party at the Election," *The Forum* 8, no. 4 (2010): 2, 15.

2. Andrew Sullivan, "Race, the Tea Party, and Conservatism," *The Daily Dish,* March 29, 2011, available at www.theatlantic.com/daily-dish /archive/2011/03/race-the-tea-party-and-conservatism/173650/.

3. Available at http://pewresearch.org/pubs/1956/tea-party-declin ing-popularity-democrats-independents-moderate-republicans. A November 2001 Pew Research Center poll showed agreement with the Tea Party among Americans at a new low of 20 percent with 27 percent disagreeing: www.people-press.org/2011/11/29more-now-disagree-with -tea-party-%e2%80%93-even-in-tea-party-districts.

4. Chris Good, "The Dwindling, Victorious Tea Party," *The Atlantic Monthly,* April 18, 2011, available at www.theatlantic.com/politics/print /2011/04/the-dwindling-victorious-tea-party/237514/. Former White House staffer Van Jones credited the Tea Party with framing the debates over carbon emissions regulation, health care, and immigration reform to the disadvantage of the Obama administration. Colin Sullivan, "Tea Party and Wonky White House Messaging Sank Cap and Trade, Van Jones Says," *New York Times,* April 6, 2011.

5. Jon Ward, "Top Tea Party Group's Goal: Stop Mitt Romney in 2012," *Huffington Post,* May 24, 2011, available at www.huffingtonpost .com/2011/05/24/romney-freedomworks-tea-party-_n_866503.html.

6. Jackie Kucinich, "Tour Will Test Mettle of Tea Party," *USA Today,* June 13, 2011.

7. Brandi Grissom, "Tea Party Sets the Agenda, and Legislators Fall in Line," *New York Times,* May 21, 2011. Driving the agenda too were two conservative political action committees, Empower Texans and Texans for Fiscal Responsibility. Legislators who did not go along with spending cuts risked retribution from these organizations.

8. Herbert J. Gans, *Middle American Individualism: The Future of Liberal Democracy* (New York: Free Press, 1988), 2.

9. Carolyn C. Jones, "Mass-Based Income Taxation: Creating a Taxpaying Culture, 1940–1952," in *Funding the Modern American State: The Rise and Fall of the Era of Easy Finance,* ed. W. Elliott Brownlee (New York: Cambridge University Press, 1996).

10. Thomas B. Edsall, "The Obama Coalition," *The Atlantic Monthly,* April 1, 2010.

11. Suzanne Mettler, "Reconstituting the Submerged State: The Challenges of Social Policy Reform in the Obama Era," *Perspectives on Politics* 8 (September 2010): 803, 811. Mettler's book is *The Submerged State: How Invisible Government Policies Undermine American Democracy* (Chicago: University of Chicago Press, 2011).

12. Suzanne Mettler, "Our Hidden Government Benefits," *New York Times,* September 19, 2011.

13. The preceding sentences are paraphrases of a slightly different formulation from John C. Diggins, *The Lost Soul of American Politics: Virtue, Self-Interest, and the Foundations of Liberalism* (New York: Basic Books, 1984), 340.

14. Mark Lilla. "The Tea Party Jacobins," *The New York Review of Books,* May 27, 2010.

15. Michael J. Sandel, *Democracy's Discontents: America in Search of a Public Philosophy* (Cambridge, MA: Harvard University Press, 1996), 3.

16. Sandel, *Democracy's Discontents,* 4–5; David H. Fischer, *Paul Revere's Ride* (New York: Oxford University Press, 1994), xvii, 28. Republican liberty requires "a knowledge of public affairs and also a sense of belonging, a concern for the whole, a moral bond with the community whose fate is at stake." Sandel, *Democracy's Discontents,* 5.

17. Sandel, *Democracy's Discontents,* 322.

18. Sandel, *Democracy's Discontents,* 323.

19. Eric Alterman, "Kabuki Democracy: Why a Progressive Presidency Is Impossible for Now," *The Nation,* July 7, 2010, available at www.thenation.com/article/37165/kabuki-democracy-why-progressive-presidency-impossible-now?page=full.

20. Stanley B. Greenberg, "Why Voters Tune Out Democrats," *New York Times,* July 30, 2011.

21. Alterman, "Kabuki Democracy," 13–14.

22. Alterman, "Kabuki Democracy," 20. "Even without the heavy overlay of right-wing propaganda, the American media as it is now constituted would be hard pressed to provide the kind of information and opportunity for debate required if the president were to undertake fundamental liberal reforms of our various dysfunctional institutions and outdated public policies." Alterman, "Kabuki Democracy," 20.

23. David E. Campbell and Robert D. Putnam, "Crashing the Tea Party," *New York Times,* August 16, 2011.

24. Karen R. Humes, Nicholas A. Jones, and Roberto R. Ramirez, "Overview of Race and Hispanic Origin: 2010," Census Bureau, March 2011, available at www.census.gov/prod/cen2010/briefs/c2010br-02.pdf.

25. Burghart and Zeskind, IREHR Report, 1, 4, 8. Hilary Shelton,

director of the NAACP's Washington bureau, said that she was "very heartened" that tea party leaders had rejected "racially inflammatory" displays. Shelton acknowledged that much of the Tea Party was "very much in tune with our democratic values, and they are actively and politically engaged." Krissah Thompson, "NAACP Watches 'Tea Party' for Racism, Stirs Controversy," *Washington Post,* September 2, 2010.

26. University of Washington Institute for the Study of Ethnicity, Race, and Sexuality (WISER), "2010 Multi-State Survey of Race and Politics," available at http://depts.washington.edu/uwiser/racepolitics.html.

27. WISER, "2011 Multi-State Survey of Race and Politics."

28. Support for Arizona's strict anti-immigrant law has been strong among some Tea Party Patriots chapters, Burghart and Zeskind, IREHR Report, 47.

29. Ronald Brownstein, "America's New Electorate," *The Atlantic Monthly,* April 1, 2011, available at www.theatlantic.com/politics/archive/2011/04/americaselectorate/73317/.

30. Brownstern, "America's New Electorate."

31. News.Max is a prominent conservative website. See Bruce Horovitz, "Marketers Profit on Sales of Tea Party Merchandise," *USA Today,* November 2, 2010; user "frankoanderson," "Fake Tea Party Groups Selling Subscriber Data to Marketers," *Blue Virginia,* April 3, 2011, available at http://bluevirginia.us/diary/3508/fake-tea-party-groups-selling-subscriber-data-to-marketers; Stephanie Mencimer, "Who Owns the Tea Party?" *Mother Jones,* April 12, 2011.

32. Kathy Kiely, "Tea Party Group Gets $1 Million Anonymous Donation," *USA Today,* September 21, 2010, available at http://content.usatoday.com/communities/onpolitics/post/2010/09/tea-party-group-gets-1-million-anonymous-donation; Stephanie Mencimer, "Tea Party Patriots Investigated: 'They Use You and Abuse You,'" *Mother Jones,* February 14, 2011; Mencimer, "Tea Party Patriots Investigated: Don't Ask, Don't Tell," *Mother Jones,* February 15, 2011.

33. Kelly Phillips Erb, "Bankrupt Tax Protester Gets Own Bailout," *Daily Finance,* October 9, 2009, available at www.dailyfinance.com/2009/10/09/bankrupt-tax-protester-gets-taxpayer-bailout/; Stephanie Mencimer, "Tea Party Patriots Investigated: The Tax Dodging Treasurer," *Mother Jones,* February 16, 2011; Beth Martin, "Tea Party Patriots Means Tea Party Profiteers to Jenny Beth Martin," *Daily Kos,* February 16, 2011, available at www.dailykos.com/story/2011/02/16/943662/-TPP-means-Tea-Party-Profiteers-to-Jenny-Beth-Martin.

Postscript. The First Tea Party

1. Benjamin Woods Labaree, *The Boston Tea Party* (New York: Oxford University Press, 1964), 18–19, 21. Labaree's classic study

provides a comprehensive understanding of events from the British and American perspectives.

2. Labaree, *Boston Tea Party,* 26–36, quotation 37.

3. Quotation from Labaree, *Boston Tea Party,* 58.

4. The preceding paragraphs are based on Labaree, *Boston Tea Party,* 125–41, quotations 134, 141.

5. Quotations are from the superb book by Alfred H. Young, *The Shoemaker and the Tea Party: Memory and the American Revolution* (Boston: Beacon Press, 1999), 42, 87, 99.

6. Young, *Shoemaker and the Tea Party,* 45.

7. Labaree, *Boston Tea Party,* 141–42. The complexities of resistance and negotiation in Massachusetts and other colonies have been lost in the necessarily truncated account here. Readers should consult Labaree and other sources for the full story.

8. On the building of insurgency throughout 1774 and 1775, see the fine recent book by T. H. Breen, *American Patriots, American Insurgents: The Revolution of the People* (New York: Hill and Wang, 2010); quotations from Young, *Shoemaker and the Tea Party,* 100, 101.

9. Adams quoted in Young, *Shoemaker and the Tea Party,* 101–2.

Index